CATHOL[OF AMERICA

Biographical Sketches of Catholic Statesmen and Political Thinkers in America's First Century, 1776–1876

Edited by
Stephen M. Krason

University Press of America,® Inc.
Lanham · Boulder · New York · Toronto · Oxford

Library of Congress Control Number: 2005938391
ISBN-13: 978-0-7618-3412-0 (paperback : alk. paper)
ISBN-10: 0-7618-3412-5 (paperback : alk. paper)

Table of Contents

Acknowledgements

Thanks are due to Franciscan University of Steubenville for financial assistance in helping to secure the publication of this book. Thanks are also due to the faculty secretarial staff at Franciscan University of Steubenville for typing assistance. The staff at Christendom Press is also to be commended for their usual outstanding job of preparing the manuscript for publication.

Preface

This book is intended to call attention to a number of important men in the history of American Catholicism and of the American nation generally. All were prominent figures in their time — some held important national political positions and/or had a significant impact on national political debate; others were better known on a regional than a national basis — but all share the curious, common fate of being largely unknown or at least not frequently thought of in our time. Their names not only do not come up often in the writing about American history and political ideas — the exception may be Roger Brooke Taney, probably the best known of the men discussed, although he is eclipsed by his predecessor as Chief Justice of the United States, the great John Marshall, and by many prominent twentieth century Supreme Court justices — but are hardly familiar even to their co-religionists of today. This is unfortunate and there may be several reasons for it, but this is not something we explore in this book. The important point to stress here — what helped to inspire this volume — is that the contributors of the essays share the conviction that the story of these men and their contributions to American political life and thought ought to be told in our time, that they deserve to receive the attention that other public men, both non-Catholics in the period focused on and Catholics in the twentieth century, have received. All of these men played a role — most an important role — in the building of the political life, thought, and institutions of the United States or part of it in our nation's formative first century. They were all, in some sense, "makers" of American political life: two in the obvious, literal sense of being numbered among our national Founding Fathers; others might be considered, in a sense, founding fathers of their states' governments because of the influence they exerted in shaping their constitutions; a few because of the ideas and learned reflection they contributed about American political life and constitutionalism; most because of their efforts in the practical political and governmental realms to make the new American institutions work.

This book occupies a somewhat unique role. There are in print individual biographies about some of the men in this volume (viz., the leading American Catholic political figures of our first century) and about other Catholics of the period who distinguished themselves in endeavors other than politics. There are also books which examine a number of prominent American Catholics of the past in various areas of life which include a few of the men written about here. None of the contributors to the present volume, however, is aware of any book, currently in print, which focuses just on a number of important Catholic statesmen or political figures of a particular period in American history, the one dealt with here or any other. The most recent book of this sort, not an anthology but the work of just one author, was J. Herman Schauinger's *Profiles in Action* (1966), which is mentioned in the bibliographies of several of the contributors. It is our hope that we might renew this effort of writers such as Schauinger to inform Americans, both Catholic and non-Catholic, about these important Catholic statesmen and political thinkers of our early history.

The figures portrayed in this volume would, without much dissent, be considered the *leading* American Catholics in the realms of active political life and political thought in the period 1776 to 1876. The book does not discuss *all* the American Catholics in these realms during this period, but is fairly comprehensive in treating the most important ones — the leading Catholics in national politics or government or who gained national, or at least substantial regional, attention because of their activity on the state level. There were other prominent Catholics who played an important public role in early

America, but who distinguished themselves in a realm other than the political (some leading military men of our first century would be an example). There were also other Catholic office-holders, but none in higher, more important positions than those included here. All except one of these men — Orestes A. Brownson — held elective or appointive public office at some time in their lives. As the essays make apparent, it is not unduly embellishing them to call them "statesmen"; all these office-holders distinguished themselves by devoted, disinterested public service with an orientation to the good of their states and nation. It is thus interesting — and something for their co-religionists of today to be proud of — that all the most prominent Catholics in politics during America's first century can reasonably and fairly be judged to have been *statesmen.*

The essays, all previously unpublished and written especially for this volume, give a good, often fairly detailed, biographical account of each man. The chief ideas of those who contributed to American political thought are also examined. Also, whenever possible, the contributors have made an attempt to discern how each man's Catholic religion influenced his public life. Limiting this volume to only figures in the first one hundred years of American history not only permits an exposition of important contributions specifically made to the building up of American politics in our nation's formative years, but also enables an objective, dispassionate assessment of their lives and efforts. Although more Catholics held important public offices in America after 1876, especially in the twentieth century, perhaps not enough time has passed to so readily permit an objective, accurate assessment of them and their contributions. A good, genuinely *historical* work, then, can be done on important people in the period this book focuses on.

These essays rely on material drawn from both original and secondary sources. The essays on Charles Carroll of Carrollton and Orestes A. Brownson — by the leading Charles Carroll scholar in America and one of the major writers on Brownson, respectively — and the one on Fitzsimons — by another leading current American Catholic historian — represent the fruits of substantial research with original source materials (done mostly for other, major works of the writers). Most of the others have leaned most heavily on secondary sources, mostly larger works on the men in question or other historical figures they were associated with, which are generally no longer readily available. There was much material on the lives and careers of some of these men; there was relatively little on others. The contributors have worked to flesh out whatever material they could to write informative, but by no means exhaustive, essays on their subjects.

Probably both scholars and laymen can find this book informative and valuable. The former — especially if they are seeking a lead-in to more substantial research or else want basic information about an important period of American Catholic history — should find in these essays an introduction to these important men which is sufficiently detailed to be useful. Each essay also includes a short bibliography which provides an avenue for further investigation. There is also an index which will enable the scholar to track down desired points quickly. Laymen should find these essays to be easily readable, substantially devoid of technical and esoteric language. Sufficient background information is generally given about the important ideas, events, and developments of this period of American history so the person who is not a professional historian or political scientist should be able to follow the narrative without difficulty. Further, the layman will not be burdened down, for the most part, with the footnote references typical of purely scholarly writing (by design, footnotes have been omitted except when preferred by a contributor). He should finish this book with a good basic knowledge of the men written about and, hopefully, a greater appreciation of the role Catholics played in shaping early American political life.

Stephen M. Krason
Steubenville, Ohio
January 20, 1993

1

Charles Carroll of Carrollton: Founding Father (1736-1832)

THOMAS O'BRIEN HANLEY

A twentieth century would-be maker of America might be discouraged or inspired by the story of Charles Carroll of Carrollton. He was the last surviving signer of the Declaration of Independence, who wrote Maryland's declaration only two days before Jefferson's committee concluded theirs. The similarities were remarkable. Carroll also served on the committee that drafted the Maryland Constitution and its Declaration of Rights.

He was then a force in moving his state toward the adoption of the Federal Constitution. He influenced the Philadelphia Convention with the spirit that ultimately led to the Bill of Rights by the first Federal Congress, where he served in the first Senate.

Remarkably, his Catholic faith and Jesuit education in France were vital forces in his career in making the America we know today with its distinguishing, constitutional structure. He may have been indirectly honored in the twentieth century by the election of John F. Kennedy. Yet he was held as a founding father for many years before he died at the age of ninety-six in 1832.

There was, however, an historic moment long before this that foretold this destiny. The conclusion of November 23, 1781 found Charles Carroll of Carrollton cherishing a memorable day.

In his Annapolis mansion he reflected on the Maryland Assembly's welcome of General George Washington, returned victorious from the Battle of Yorktown. Although the final details of American Independence won by the war were not complete, the life of the Maryland republic and her twelve sister states was thriving. The presence of the honored leader in the Annapolis chamber symbolized not only their victory, but a union now enlarged in spirit beyond the war-time dimensions of the Articles of Confederation. At the center of the emerging Legend of the Revolution begun that day was the prudent, virtuous and courageous citizen from nearby Mount Vernon. He was destined to preside in the near future over a national republic.

This was indeed the implication of the address of Charles Carroll that memorable day in the assembly. The leader from Yorktown was welcomed with "gratitude," but enlarged with "veneration." The revolutionary experience under him, they said, "raised the drooping spirits of your country." Not only was Washington already revered as the "Father of his country," he had at this early date symbolized the union of the thirteen republics as now a single country. In the language of Carroll's father and generally throughout the thirteen states *country* was usually used as a reference to one's own state. The address of Carroll and his associates meant that all became a single country under a divine guidance: "a rational ground of belief, that under the favour of Divine Providence, the freedom, independence and happiness of America will shortly be established upon the surest foundations."

In response to these words, General Washington found a call to love and serve that country which emerged from the revolutionary ordeal. This was a demand equal, he believed, to the "exertions which have already so greatly humbled the power of our inveterate enemies." In the quiet of his study, Charles Carroll of Carrollton could reflect on this new prompting in the wellsprings of patriotic ambition. He relished the recollection of standing with the "Father of his Country" on that eventful day.

So, too, his place among the signers of the Declaration of Independence, which patriotic artists were already beginning to portray for posterity, came to mind. It assured him he was with Washington and these other statesmen in the revolutionary legend now being woven.

In his Maryland he saw a challenge to help bring her into the unfolding life of America, his country. A founding father of the Maryland Constitution, he understood that a new creation was needed. His Classical Republicanism was a guide in 1776 and it would yield enlightenment in the creative work ahead. Hopefully he would find a place in that phase of the American legend, a reward in his later years of reflection. Indeed, the Maryland Senator was already aware of the limitations in the Maryland republican constitution; and it reminded him of the need for growth and revision of the 1776 interpretation of the ideal. His committee's address and Washington's response held a sketch of these expectations for the decade that was only beginning.

In the midst of these thoughts about the future were others recollecting the years immediately following 1776. Moving about his mansion in this mood, the portraits on its walls reminded him of his family legend as well as his country's. It took on new depth and detail with the revolutionary legend he saw unfolding before him. The primary figure was found in Englehardt Kuhn's characterization of Charles Carroll the Settler and Attorney General of Lord Baltimore. His pursuit of religious freedom in Maryland was undone by the Protestant Revolution in 1688, only shortly after he had settled the landed estate given by Lord Baltimore. The Attorney Generalship was taken from the man whom Kuhn had donned with the symbols of Inner Temple, where he had studied English law under its masters.

Charles Carroll of Carrollton now stood before a great and courageous grandfather, without whom he would not have the inheritance which opened the way to this eventful moment. Placed with this painting of his great forebear was Sir Joshua

Reynolds' of himself. Young Charles Carroll of Carrollton, however, was without his forebear's robes of Inner Temple, a privation endured for his faith. An education in law nearby it and on the continent compensated for any limitation in his legal studies. He had a special advantage in a philosophical education at the Jesuit College of Louis the Great in Paris and in the other liberal arts at their other institutions in France. The family tradition for this was another debt of Charles Carroll of Carrollton to the founder of the family legend. The Maryland Senator and constitutionalist felt no sense of superiority, but of indebtedness and a call to further achievements to honor such a forebear.

The troubled life of the rejected Attorney General of Lord Baltimore settled on his son, Charles Carroll of Annapolis, along with an enlarged estate. This father of Charles Carroll of Carrollton responded with the ambition that now marked the family legend. Denied public worship, his mansions provided chapels for his beleaguered Catholic neighbors and a residence for the Jesuit chaplains. With other Catholic gentlemen he drew up a petition to Lord Baltimore recalling him to a dedication to religious freedom expressed in the first Maryland Assembly in 1639. In time he grew weary with failures in these efforts and considered moving to Louisiana under French Catholic auspices. His son, however, was soon to return to Maryland. His studies on the continent fused with the growing Catholic tradition of freedom in Maryland, as they did with the law learned in London. Once in Maryland again, young Charles Carroll of Carrollton continued his legal reflection in the context of English constitutional thought. He moved to this new ground in hopes of serving his community and provincial society in pursuit of freedom.

Before young Charles left England, he had visited Lord Baltimore and reasserted his father's case for religious liberty, but framed it in the broader rights of Englishmen in a colony. The Assembly's double tax on Catholics, he said, "was subversive of the Maryland Constitution." In this imaginative vein were the seeds of Carroll's future growth into the Maryland Declaration of Independence and Constitution from his hands. It was in this strong fabric that his father's aspirations for the Anglo-Irish Catholic community could vindicate their rights so long denied. Returning from England at the age of twenty-eight, the family legend enhanced his growing sureness of identity. This prepared him for the mature life of achievements of his own in playing a significant role in establishing the Maryland Republic. Such fulfillment, he surely understood, was a vindication of his father and grandfather, who had lived heroically without the satisfactions he was experiencing during these years.

His emerging self-identity in this area was disturbed in another touching his affective life. While in England he had courted Louisa Baker, who turned away from him. Returned to American he was engaged to Rachel Cooke, who died shortly before the marriage was to take place. In time he married Mary Darnall, whose widowed mother and she were given the permanent hospitality of Doughoregan Manor. Her father had been executed for an embezzlement and the disturbed household emotionally affected her subsequent life with her husband in his destiny for public life.

The St. Francis de Sales' spiritual ideal of Carroll's community sought to balance the aggressiveness of the Christian gentleman with a tenderness in his personal life. The author of a treatise on the love of God instructed the Maryland Catholic community on its extension into the family. His father had put his seal of approval on the Cooke marriage and the legal competence of his son to receive the family inheritance by force of Governor Sharpe's authorization, needed by Catholics. This was not the case with his own marriage, which was only certified by a Catholic priest according to the norms for a mission country.

In time Charles grew to love Molly Darnall. Despite her disturbed background in her father's case, she delighted in entertainments at the side of her staid husband. While two of her children did not survive infancy, two daughters did. So did her only son, who would be known as Charles Carroll of Homewood, after his future Baltimore estate.

The ceremonial meeting with George Washington brought these reflections on his early life and the Revolutionary War. At an even deeper level he reconsidered his constitutional service to Maryland and her sister republics. On the larger scene, the Continental Congress created the Declaration of Independence, which he signed for his own state. Two days before that document from the hand of Thomas Jefferson and his committee, he had written Maryland's declaration for the Assembly. This empowered him to act for the state in signing the document at Philadelphia. The similarity of the two declarations of human freedom is remarkable in their understanding of John Locke. Yet the Marylander clearly shows the influence of his years of study on the continent at Jesuit colleges. While at the College of Louis the Great in Paris, his father at considerable expense managed to get Locke's writings to him. In the spirit of the Enlightenment's understanding of the dignity of the human person, the college counteracted the Jansenistic and Puritan interpretation of the fall of Adam. Stuart kings were declaring a direct communication of civil authority from God in the spirit of these understandings. In his philosophical studies in Paris the young Marylander took up a contrary reasoning found in Robert Bellarmine and Francisco Suarez. In them the integrity of human nature espoused by Thomas Aquinas was carried into the social realm: civil authority was from God placed in the people.

The implications were crucial to the subsequent career of Maryland's constitutionalist and a member of its Senate for years to come. Man as created in God's image and likeness had within his nature the source of civil authority. Carroll's declaration, as Jefferson's, cites this source of civil authority to justify America's war for independence. Against this background Carroll's declaration demanded that Americans "be exempted from Parliamentary taxation." "To regulate their internal government and polity," he continued, "the people of this Colony have ever considered as their inherent and unalienable right." The implications of this were clear, for "without the former they can have no property, without the latter, no security in their lives or liberties." He pitted the right given by God to the people, who spoke through their chosen representatives, against the arrogant claims of kings. "We the Delegates of Maryland in convention assembled," he continued, "do declare that the King of G[reat] B[ritain] has violated his compact with the People and that they owe no allegiance to him."

The voice of this authority in the future of the new nation, however, required a painstaking statecraft in the construction of the state constitutions and the Articles of Confederation. It was in this role that Charles Carroll of Carrollton again distinguished himself as he drew on his Catholic education as well as the classic authors Jefferson had mastered. He had advanced through the stages found in Jesuit schools: grammar, rhetoric, Classical Greek and Roman Languages and Literature. From it he had by 1776 distilled an understanding of Classical Roman Republicanism, which emphasized the eminence of the Senate in securing the rights and well-being of the citizens from whom their authority derived. In this spirit Cicero had styled that body: *Senatus pupulusque Romani*, "The Senate and the People of Rome" who spoke through it. Carroll always understood, however, that this was not the democracy of the Greek city states. Rather, the august body would protect the people against demagogues and even themselves in a moment of a hasty, ill-advised public policy by a directly elected lower house.

On the committee to draft Maryland's Constitution, Charles Carroll of Carrollton implanted these ideas in the background of the growing American Nation. The need of a federal union to replace that of the Articles of Confederation had come forward in Carroll's mind ahead of most Americans. He was concerned for and reflected on the proper form of a federal constitution.

Following the departure of General Washington from

Annapolis for Mount Vernon, Carroll turned to this challenge of
a true Nation of a United States under a Federal Constitution.
Immediately at hand in 1782 was a preliminary step toward this in
the Maryland Assembly. It witnessed Carroll's hostile conflict
with Samuel Chase. The member of the House of Delegates had
not understood the Senate as Carroll had designed it in the
state's constitution. Nor had Chase reconciled self-interest with
popular election. In time he manipulated the latter for the
benefit of the former. Such a debtor promoted the escalation of
inflation in money issues and other ways. Carroll saw America's
growing economy as a force leading to a truly federal government
of all the American people and their states. He hoped that it
would lift the state assemblies above their limitations seen in the
Chase episodes.

The critical situation in Maryland kept him from attending
the Federal Constitutional Convention in Philadelphia. His
cousin Daniel Carroll (brother of the first Catholic Bishop, John
Carroll) was elected as Maryland's delegate. To him Charles
entrusted his "Plan of Government." The document of several
pages applied Carroll's understanding of Locke. Carroll called
for the election of members of the Senate by the state assemblies
as a process of refined representation. Daniel Carroll
collaborated with James Wilson of Pennsylvania on many aspects
of these problems and particularly on the office of president.

Here Charles Carroll's "Plan of Government" called for his
election by the Congress, in keeping with his principle of refined
representation. As the debate in Philadelphia unfolded on this
matter, Daniel Carroll supported the direct election of the
president by the voter, but mediated by an electoral college.
Such a process Charles Carroll had originated for the Maryland
Constitution in its provision for the election of members of the
Senate. In another area of what would become the Bill of Rights
after ratification of the Constitution by the states, both Charles
and Daniel Carroll took the lead. Maryland delegate Luther
Martin called for profession of belief in Christianity by federal

office holders, which the Carrolls opposed.

This was related to Carroll's view in Maryland's Constitution where he had provided for human rights in Article Seven of the Declaration of Rights. It secured the citizen against "any injury done to him in his person and property." "Civil societies and governments," he reasoned, "were principally instituted for the security of property and the protection of personal liberty."

In the general outcome at Philadelphia he was more than satisfied and urged its ratification without amendments. He failed, however, to secure a seat in the state's Ratifying Convention, thanks to the action of Chase and his other political opponents. Yet Carroll effectively turned to the press and the impetus for ratification triumphed. Charles Carroll of Carrollton appropriately was elected Maryland's first United States Senator. In the first Congress he had the satisfaction of seeing the Bill of Rights passed. The First Amendment, he was pleased to see, carried the spirit of his own Maryland declaration for religious and other personal freedom. Maryland was the second state to ratify the Bill of Rights, which was appropriate from the standpoint of Catholics, as Carroll felt. The establishment of religion prohibition in it would in time end Maryland's requirement that office holders profess belief in Christianity. This was a provision Carroll opposed based on the Catholic tradition begun in the first Maryland assembly.

A Maryland law was soon passed which made Carroll choose to sit in only one Senate. In relinquishing his Federal seat, however, he felt that he could better serve the new government by leading his state into a firmer bond of union.

Charles Carroll of Carrollton continued to lead his state in economic growth. Moving beyond a planter's estate and other land amounting to thousands of acres, some in Pennsylvania, he enlarged the Baltimore Iron Works his father had initiated. Learning from the textile industry in New England, he soon had fullers at Doughoregan weaving cloth. In time Baltimore had its textile industry. He advocated manumission of slaves in the economic context. They were prepared for carpentry and other crafts and often found a place in Baltimore's black community, now enlarged by migrants from the Caribbean. He advocated an assembly bill which would promote a factory in the New England design. Manumitted women would there find income to support their independence.

Proud of his Irish heritage, he adapted his plantation practices to the growing number of immigrants from there by 1820. He promoted indentured servitude in their case, covering their passage from Ireland and granting the seven years of service on his land. Some chose to stay on working the small acreage they had been granted and in time with Carroll's agreement bought additional land. Many of these immigrants were encouraged to learn a trade and they found their place in Baltimore, where St. Patrick's parish would soon be founded.

Several years before the Federal Constitution, he had embarked on a long career in canal construction, which ultimately led him into the national scene with the Baltimore and Ohio Railroad, of which he would become director. George Washington had earlier been drawn into these movements toward a national transportation system, after Carroll's earlier planning for a canal from the Susquehanna River into Maryland to the area of Frederick and Doughoregan Manor. This in time was put aside for establishing the Chesapeake and Potomac Canal, in which Washington was a partner and for which Carroll had secured capital. It was enlarged progressively by these developments. He was an early investor in the Bank of the United States and a source for loans, George Washington being among applicants. Called by the first President of the United States, "the most monied man in America," Carroll was forthright in advancing a national economy, which strengthened the union of the states he had helped by his role in the Federal Constitution.

From the beginning of the Republic, Carroll used his

position and wealth to advance higher education. His efforts in the founding of Washington College and the growth of St. John's in Annapolis were in keeping with his ideal of an educated citizenry, particularly in the case of its representatives in government. Archbishop John Carroll looked to him in making a Catholic contribution to this need of the Republic. As something like a trustee, he received money from others to add to his own in establishing the College of Georgetown in an ecumenical spirit as related to the other colleges.

Charles Carroll of Carrollton, the revolutionary gentleman and statesman, now stood as a Founding Father in the eyes of the nations' younger leaders. When Thomas Jefferson and John Adams died in 1826, this was more the case, for he was the last surviving signer of the Declaration of Independence. His Catholic community, native, Irish and French, took pride and assurance at this. In the face of anti-Catholic Nativism in this era he was indeed a leader in the Church. This was particularly so after the death of his cousin, Archbishop John Carroll in 1825.

His faith and its community strengthened him in this service and in his devotion to his family in its sorrows. These began in 1782 with the death of his wife and child. Her single aunt at a sacrifice took her place in the care of the children. Young Charles would go abroad for his education, but his return led to many disappointments for the father, as the son ultimately succumbed to alcoholism. His two daughters, however, also educated in France, married men who were leaders of their time: Richard Caton managed Carroll's estate and growing enterprises; and Robert Goodloe Harper debated Daniel Webster in the United States Senate. These personal satisfactions enlarged his enjoyment of the public ones as the Catholic Founder.

Perhaps at the present time there is a special message to Americans here. As the twentieth century draws to a close, there is growing ambition to create an educated life in the service of a country that triumphed in the rise of capitalism in industry, service corporations and investment wealth, corporate and

private.   These leaders have Carroll's energy, if not his
disciplined "habit of business."   Carroll had his library and
understood the role of leisure in a worthy Christian life of
intelligence that would also serve others.   He did not feel guilty
about being "the most monied man in America."   St. Francis de
Sales, in his *Introduction to the Devout Life*," schooled him in the
love of God.   While it provided security, it reminded him that this
was to make it possible for him to serve others less fortunate and
be a leader of society towards a Christian ideal.

The American Founder integrated his faith and its
community into that role which history has preserved as a
challenge to all ages.

Bibliography

Thomas O'Brien Hanley, S.J.,   *Charles Carroll of Carrollton: The
Making of a Revolutionary Gentleman* (Washington, DC: Catholic
University of America Press, 1970); *Their Rights and Liberties:
The Beginnings of Religious and Political Freedom in Maryland*
(Chicago: Loyola University Press, 1984).

2

Daniel Carroll: Merchant-Planter and Founding Father (1730-1796)

JOHN J. CARRIGG

Daniel Carroll was not as famous as his illustrious cousin Charles Carroll of Carrollton or as well known as his brother John, the first Archbishop of Baltimore and founder of Georgetown University, yet he played a leading role in the politics of the American Revolution and the foundation of the United States of America. He signed the Articles of Confederation and the Constitution. He was a member of the Maryland Executive Council and the Maryland Senate. He served in the first term of the United States Congress as a member of the House and was appointed by President Washington to the commission responsible for the formation of the District of Columbia. The history of Maryland as a new state under the Articles and the Constitution is unthinkable without Daniel Carroll. He is singular as one of the few Catholics who played a role in the politics of this period, remaining loyal to the Church although perhaps driven by the overwhelming Protestant complexion of the time to an ecumenical stance far ahead of his time.

He was born to wealth inheriting from his father and mother wide acres in Maryland, expanding all this by marriage and a bequest from his brother John, the Jesuit who turned over his property to Daniel on entering the Society of Jesus. As a large landholder he shared the aristocratic view of the class but with a curious democratic admixture and on most points stood for a strong national government. He was a merchant importer who maintained important connections with firms in England and Scotland. Plagued by ill health which he tried to correct by diet and exercise he often dragged himself to meetings where his presence was necessary. A slaveholder, the second largest in Frederick county, Maryland, he was widowed at an early age and stayed single the rest of his life living with his son and daughter, his servants and slaves on his estate, when he wasn't at Annapolis, Philadelphia or New York on his country's business. Regrettably the written records on Daniel Carroll are relatively scanty. He kept no diary, most of the letters he wrote have perished. He was appointed to many committees while a State Senator but the minutes of their activities and Carroll's role in them are often sketchy and sometimes non-existent. He made no unforgettable utterances that ring down through the ages. Most of the statements attributed to him are solid but not exciting. Yet he was well thought of by his peers, for he received many important assignments of trust and responsibility, most notably his appointment to the Confederation Congress and the Constitutional Convention and finally to the United States Congress. It is difficult to determine how the Carrolls amassed so much wealth being both Irish and Catholic in 17th and 18th century Great Britain. Most likely the Calvert connection is a partial explanation plus the Carroll drive, brains and superior education. With wealth came influence and this Daniel Carroll used effectively in the interest of his country. Given the paucity of information on the man, we have to settle for William Pierce's brief summary: "Daniel Carroll is a man of large fortune and influence in his State. He possesses plain good sense and is in the full confidence in his countrymen."

Writing about Daniel Carroll, one soon find himself in a maze of Daniel and Charles Carrolls. There are many of each in

18th century Maryland and outstanding historians have blundered in trying to sort them out. There are two distinct Carroll lines, the one founded by Charles Carroll the Attorney General who came to Maryland in 1688. His son Charles Carroll of Annapolis was the father of the famous Charles Carroll of Carrollton. The other line was founded by a certain Keane Carroll of Ireland who never set foot in America. His son Daniel Carroll immigrated to Maryland around 1720. He married a very famous beauty, Eleanor Darnell whose grandfather was the brother-in-law of Lord Baltimore. They were the parents of Daniel Carroll II, the subject of this study. He married Eleanor Carroll who was first cousin of Charles Carroll of Carrollton, thus joining the two lines. Daniel and Eleanor Carroll had a son Daniel Carroll III and they also had a nephew Daniel Carroll of Duddington who was the son of his wife's brother Charles Carroll.

Daniel Carroll II is also known as Daniel Carroll of Upper Marlborough, Daniel Carroll of Rock Creek, Daniel Carroll the Signer and Daniel Carroll the Commissioner.

The image of Maryland as a haven for persecuted Catholics and the first colony to grant religious freedom to its citizens lingers on to those with a general outline of American history. Hence it is ironic on closer scrutiny to find that Maryland after the revolution of 1688 was the locus of vehement anti-Catholic legislation. Catholics were not permitted to educate their children in the Faith, Catholic Churches were not permitted, Catholics could not vote or hold office and finally Catholics were subjected to double taxation. All this came about with the growing Protestant population of Maryland and the tide of anti-Catholic feeling in the wake of the Glorious Revolution. A number of prominent Catholics apostatized, the most distinguished being the fourth Lord Baltimore Benedict who became an Anglican, which was the established Church in Maryland. But Daniel Carroll II kept the Faith of his Fathers and it might be added of his mother Eleanor Darnell, a most pious Catholic whose grandfather has been described by one authority as "a violent Jacobite, an unbending recusant, and a kinsman of the Calverts."

Daniel Carroll II was first taught by his mother who had received a fine education abroad and perhaps by an Irish tutor, free or indentured who was usually disguised as a laborer to avoid the fine of 40 shillers a day levied the head of the household for employing a Catholic tutor. Richard Purcell suggests that the laws were probably more severe than their enforcement under an Anglo Saxon system of government.

A tribute to his parents' staunch Catholicism was their determination to give their son the best in Catholic education and so in 1742 at age twelve Daniel Carroll was sent on a perilous voyage across the ocean to study at the Jesuit College of St. Omer in French Flanders. Here from the English Jesuit Fathers he learned Latin and French and some Greek plus Philosophy and Theology and no doubt imbibed the conservative view of his teachers. A minor irony but interesting is the fact that Great Britain and her colonies were at war with France (King George's War) during the period that Daniel Carroll was matriculating in the enemy country.

Sending a child abroad for a Catholic education violated another Maryland law:

> Whoever shall be convicted of sending any child, or other person beyond the seas, out of the King's obedience to the intent that such a child or person shall be educated in the Roman Religion, shall forfeit f100 for the sole use and benefit of him who shall discover any person so offending to the end that Protestant children may not in the life time of their parents, for want of fitting maintenance, be necessitated in compliance with their parents to embrace the Popish religion.

The year Daniel Carroll returned to Maryland (1748) his brother John, the future priest, and his cousin Charles crossed the ocean to join the ranks of exiled scholars at St. Omer's . . .

training in the *ratio studiorum*.

John Gilmary Shea describes the effects of this European training on the young Americans who were sent to St. Omer's:

> The effect of this continental education on the young Catholic gentlemen was clearly seen. As a class, they were far superior to their Protestant neighbors, who, educated at home, were narrow and insular in their ideas, ignorant of modern languages, and all that was going on beyond their county limits and its fox hunts and races. The Catholic on the contrary, was conversant with several languages, with the current literature of Europe, the science of the day, with art and the great galleries where the masterpieces of painting and sculpture could be seen. He returned to England or his colonial home after forming acquaintance with persons of distinction and influence, whose correspondence retained and enlarged the knowledge he had acquired.

Within three years of returning home, Daniel Carroll's father died (1751) and responsibility for managing the family estate and mercantile business fell on the only son (his brother John having stayed in Europe to study for the priesthood).

Having inherited from his father 5000 acres and an additional 3000 acres which he owned jointly with his brother John (who gave up his share on entering the priesthood in 1771), he received a handsome wedding gift from his wife Eleanor Carroll of 300 pounds cash. In the years ahead he engaged in extensive real estate transactions buying and selling hundreds of acres of Maryland farm land.

One letter from Daniel Carroll exists in this period. It was written in 1762 to an inquiring kinsman, James Carroll of Ireland and provides valuable information on the Carroll geneology. Of the original family of three boys and four girls, six lived till the death of their father in 1751, while the oldest, Henry, drowned as a child. Daniel, the oldest surviving son, married Eleanor Carroll, a daughter of Ann Rozier of Cerne Abbey, England, thereby connecting more closely the Charles Carroll of

Carrollton Branch to that of the Carrolls of Upper Marlborough, Maryland. His brother John became a Jesuit priest in 1769 (and later in 1790, became Bishop of Baltimore and in 1808 was elevated to the rank of Archbishop). A sister, Ann, married Robert Brent of Virginia. Eleanor, the fifth child, married William Brent, Jr. Mary, the next in line, was the wife of Notley Young, and the youngest, Elizabeth, never married. She lived with her mother in Forest Glen and on the death of her mother acquired all her personal and real property.

One other letter surviving from an otherwise sketchy historical period, was written to Daniel Carroll on 1764 by John Carroll who was then in Liege studying for the priesthood. He complained that he had not heard from home in over a year and if it weren't for word from an uncle he would not know whether his friends were alive or dead. Now that the war was over he expected a greater flow of news from home but that hadn't been the case. He was sending this letter by way of Charles Carroll of Carrollton who was completing his studies in London and heading home. He had heard that Daniel planned to come to Europe and he looked forward to seeing him again. Finally he suggested that any mail should be addressed to Mr. Poyntz with Mr. Wright, Banker, Henriette Street, Convent Garden, London. He closed with this poignant line: "I am at loss for want of letters from you whom to apply to for money this year. Write as soon as possible and believe me to be, Dear Brother, your most affectionate brother John Carroll."

The record is silent on Daniel Carroll's role in the important events that led to the break with Great Britain during the 1760's and '70's. We do know that his store handled a wide variety of goods judging by the purchases he made from the Scotch firms, located in Upper Marlborough. An inventory of purchases made in the years 1762-1764 included the following items: rum, saddle cloths, nails, padlocks, knee beeches, slates, loaf sugar, worsted hose, thread, shoes, rope, colored ribbons, yarn stockings, box candles and crimson vest buttons. Payment was accepted in currency, bills of credit or tobacco. The non-importation agreements adopted by the colonies must have hurt his business seriously, but judging by his future conduct we can be certain that he was on the side of the Patriots.

He was also busy managing his vast acres and buying and selling real estate. The lands he inherited from his father, mother, brother and wife were expanded by additional purchases totalling 1,680 acres. At the same time he sold off some of his inheritance in the amount of 2,300 acres. Later, during the 1780's he purchased a large amount of confiscated loyalist property, particularly in Baltimore. It is interesting to note that Charles Carroll of Carrollton did not buy such property.

Daniel Carroll also invested in Maryland and Pennsylvania securities which paid handsome profits when exchanged for United States certificates under Hamilton's funding system.

He also owned stock in two land companies, the Mississippi and the Potomac.

Finally, he bought and sold negro slaves as indicated from this advertisement in the *Maryland Gazette*:

> To be sold to the highest bidder: Sixteen Country born slaves, consisting of one young fellow, several women, boys and girls, among them a good cook wench, two women brought up to waiting in a family... Sale begins at three o'clock in Prince George's County Courthouse.

and this:

> From William Lock Weems purchases were made of negro slaves. (Dublin, Violette, Charles, Bock and Primus), furniture and stock of horses, cattle, sheep, hogs, and a barrel of flour and Indian corn. In almost all purchases young negroes were bought, one as young as eight years of age with his mother, Hester, and his Father, Bab, for thirty-eight pounds, eighteen shillings, nine pence and three farthings, or a child eleven years of age named Stephen with his mother, Margery (29 yrs.), [father] Bambo (35 yrs.) for a sum of fifty pounds currency.

Daniel Carroll was interested in helping recent immigrants from Ireland get settled in America. In 1774 he wrote a letter to Washington describing his efforts on behalf of such immigrants:

> In the winter 1771, I received a letter from a Merchant of my acquaintance in Galway in Ireland, strongly recommending some Irish families who had embarked for America. These poor people, finding they could not live under the action of their landlord ... were able to pay their passages and bring with them some family goods and working utensils ... They have had room and firing on my land since their arrival. The men have worked abroad and by their conduct justified the recommendations given of them and I am certain will be of singular service, wherever they settle, particularly in working meadows ... It would not, I apprehend, be bad policy in those who may possess large bodies or tracts of land to lay out a Glebe for a Clergyman. This would have considerable weight with many Irish Roman Catholics who would probably bring their own Clergymen with them. I intend myself taking a trip into these new Countries, as they are called and purchasing some lands if the terms and title were agreeable in hopes of making it turn to advantage, as my connections are in Ireland ... Should matters be settled time enough this fall, I shall put my resolution into execution.

Why he wrote this letter to Washington is a bit of a puzzle unless he wanted to interest Washington in the idea of promoting immigration to America; but would Washington be interested in promoting Irish Catholic immigration? It seems doubtful.

In other ways Daniel Carroll supported the Catholic cause. He maintained St. John's chapel in Rock Creek out of his own pocket until his brother, John was able to support it out of diocesan funds. He paid the tuition of his two grandsons at Georgetown University, Joseph and Patrick Sims both children of his daughter Mary who was the wife of Col. Patrick Sims.

In the codicil of his will two acres of land was to be given to "John Carroll and his successors ... comprehending and contiguous to the Roman Catholic Congregation worshipping therein which two acres are to be laid of by my trustees in my will mentioned."

Daniel Carroll's first public role occurred in 1756 when Governor Lee appointed him to serve as interpreter on a joint Maryland-Virginia commission to negotiate with the Catawba and Cherokee Indians to secure "their friendship and active assistance" against the French. Carroll lived on land adjacent to these tribes and apparently had learned their language. Governor Dinwiddie of Virginia, thought highly of Carroll and said "he is a person of credit and you may believe what he says." This brief stint as interpreter was a minor departure from his customary role of merchant and land-owner.

The American Revolution and the State Constitution of Maryland (1776) gave Catholics the right to vote, within property qualifications, and to serve their state in a political capacity. These changes paved the way for the appointment of Daniel Carroll to the Maryland State Council. Members of this five man body were chosen by both houses of the Maryland Assembly. They were to be above 25 years of age and "most sensible, discreet and experienced possessing lands above the value of 1000 pounds of current money." In addition, all public office holders had to declare their belief in the Christian religion, a declaration easily made by the strong Catholic Carroll.

To this Council Daniel Carroll, now described as of "Rock Creek," was renamed in 1778, 1779 and 1780. The State Council assisted the Governor and was in control of the military forces of the state, the raising of supplies and foodstuffs and finances. Carroll was one of the most regular members of the Council, missing very few meetings. Providing salt, sugar, flour, clothing and arms for the Maryland troops absorbed most of his time while in the Council. Securing these supplies was made extremely difficult by the lack of sound money in the country. The currency was highly inflated, pay to members of the Council was in near worthless currency when paid at all. The service was really a gift to the public and many who were appointed refused to serve. Carroll held on grimly through four years when he was appointed to the Continental Congress in 1781.

In the same year he received another honor from his state when he was chosen by the Electoral College as one of the fifteen Senators of Maryland to represent the western shore for Prince George's County. He was to serve for a five year term beginning in 1781. While in the Senate he served with his cousin Charles Carroll of Carrollton. Three times he was elected President of the Maryland Senate. During the years 1781-1785 he was a very busy politician dividing his duties between the Maryland Senate and the United States Congress. Maryland held out stubbornly against ratifying the Articles of Confederation until the western lands were given up to the national government. When early in 1781 Virginia yielded up her lands west of the Ohio, Maryland agreed to join the Articles and Daniel Carroll was chosen by the Maryland legislature to sit in the Congress along with Daniel of St. Thomas Jennifer, John Hanson and Richard Potts.

There was great rejoicing in Philadelphia when on March 1, 1781 Carroll joined his colleague John Hanson in signing the Articles of Confederation ending Maryland's holdout and legitimizing the national government. To quote Samuel Eliot Morison: "The Church bells of Philadelphia pealed the good news; sloop-of-war *Ariel*, commanded by John Paul Jones, dressed ship and fired a 21 gun salute; Samuel Huntington, president of Congress, gave a reception and the evening was ushered in by an elegant exhibition of fireworks."

The only Catholic among the 48 signers, Carroll was in good company with such worthies as Oliver Wolcott, Gouverneur Morris, Roger Sherman, Elbridge Gerry, John Witherspoon, Robert Morris, Joseph Reed, John Dickinson, Richard Henry Lee, John Penn, Francis Lightfoot Lee and Henry Laurens . . . all of whom were to go on to prominent places in the founding of the American Republic.

Money was the chief concern of Carroll and the Maryland

delegation during his three year term with the Congress under the Articles. There was very little money to pay the troops, to purchase supplies or provide for the salaries of the Congressmen. Carroll and his colleagues were constantly after the governor of Maryland to correct the situation. "We hope an ample supply will be forwarded without which it is impossible to remain here." Carroll wrote to Governor Paca in March of 1783. "We have been reduced to the humiliating circumstances of attempting to borrow without success," he wrote another time. And again: "it is not in our power to continue here without ... some other Mode of Supply than that of Paper Money." At one point Carroll told the Governor that he was returning the money sent to him by the state because "we can make no use of it here." The Governor's reply wasn't very comforting: the Treasury is exhausted and "it is not in our power to supply you with any Money." It is hard to believe but Carroll, who was periodically ill during this stay in Philadelphia, refused to call a doctor "because he had not Money to pay him for his visit and Medics." Governor Paca hoping for an improvement in the state's financial affairs wrote to the finance officer:

> The Delegates in Congress inform us by every Opportunity, of their very great Distress for money ... This situation is truly disgraceful to the state, as well as to the Gentlemen who represent it, and we request you will immediately take Measures to supply them with a Sum equal to what will be due to them by the time the Remittance reaches Philadelphia ... We need not urge any reasons to convince you of the impropriety of Delay.

A week later Paca received an angry note from the Maryland delegation in Philadelphia:

> The Bill of 300 pounds which the Intendant gave Mr. Carroll reason to expect by the Post of last week, is not received and when it is, will not be adequate to our claims or necessities. The extravagance of living in this place and the great scarcity of money said to be felt by all, and by us in

particular, reduces us to the distressing alternative of leaving Congress or subsisting, at the expense of a Class of People who cannot afford to give a credit.

The government under the Articles could not tax, it could only request funds from the states which never furnished the amount needed so the government resorted to the printing press and its notes soon became worthless whereupon a new issue was authorized and the cycle was repeated. Daniel Carroll favored a 5% impost on goods imported into the country and so did every state in the Confederation except Rhode Island and that state defeated the measure which would have gone part of the way in alleviating the financial distress. Daniel Carroll at the prompting of Robert Morris sent out a plea to all the states to contribute to the support of the government:

> This inattention in the state has almost endangered our very existence as a People, and altho' it is our duty to acknowledge with gratitude the many interpositions of Providence ... yet to expect the assistance of Heaven, without using all the means in our power is rather mockery than religion, and to rely on foreign aid without preparing to cooperate with it, is betraying equally our interests and honor.
> The special and peculiar circumstances of the present moment require(s our attention). The restoration of public credit, the expediting business, the checking extravagance, and introducing economy into the public expenditures were the objects which Congress had in view in the establishment of a Superintendent General of Finance ... it depends upon the State to render them permanent and effectual.
> (We) entreat ... a speedy and close attention ... being firmly persuaded that nothing but a punctual compliance and requisitions both of man and money for the current year will enable us to do (it) ...

Carroll served on several committees that dealt with the problem of feeding captured British troops. Since feeding the Continental army was straining the resources of the Congress there was very little left for feeding British troops. Carroll told the governor that keeping these prisoners was causing great difficulties for the states "because the greater part of these troops will escape before some Effectual measures can be adopted to have them supplied with Provisions."

The prisoners were returned to Great Britain after the Treaty of Paris was ratified in January of 1784.

How to compensate the officers discharged from the service as the war wound down was another problem for Congress. One proposal was that these officers receive a pension of half pay for life. Carroll favored full pay for five years. The question had not been resolved when he left Congress although his motion that soldiers be given a furlough with a promise that discharge would follow on the conclusion of peace was adopted by the Congress unanimously.

Carroll was ill when Congress was decoding the question of instructions to the Paris peace delegation and for want of Maryland's vote the "moderate boundaries" position failed. Carroll dragged himself to the Assembly and voted in favor of the so-called moderate position and that position was adopted.

Luzerene, the French minister to Philadelphia, was very pleased to see Carroll return to Congress and vote the moderate position. It apparently had little effect, for the British in the final peace gave the Americans a most generous settlement on the boundary question, particularly as they occupied a score of key points within those boundaries.

On another interesting point, Carroll took a position that would make him very unpopular with his colleagues. Since Congress was often frustrated by a lack of quorum, Carroll proposed a motion that "every morning at 11 o'clock an account be taken, together with an account of the states unrepresentation, be sent to the Executive of each state."

Lack of pay caused a group of unruly soldiers to demonstrate against the Congress on June 21, 1783 and President Elias Boudinot decided to move the government to Princeton

rather than stay in Philadelphia and put up with such a
"disorderly and menacing" crowd. Immediately other cities
offered to accommodate Congress and McHenry and Daniel
Carroll pushed Annapolis as an ideal site for future meetings. By
the time Congress met there in the Fall of '83 Carroll was no
longer a member of the Maryland delegation. He finished his
term in November of 1783.

He now returned to Maryland to take up his duties in the
Senate. Six months after being elected to the Senate he took the
oath of office by declaring his belief in the Christian religion.
The term was five years. His attendance was spotty during the
first two years, since he spent most of his time in Philadelphia
with the Congress. The Maryland Senate was a very aristocratic
conservative body, consisting of 15 members chosen by an
Electoral College. Daniel Carroll would join his cousin Charles
of Carrollton in this distinguished group. Three times he was
chosen President of the Senate and was elected to two full terms.

Carroll was a member of a committee appointed by the
Senate to instruct the commissioners on the Potomac company
canal route that was designed to connect the source of the
Potomac with the Ohio River and thus tie the eastern shore with
the western country. He purchased stock in the company and
presided over meetings held in 1784 and 1785.

While president of the Senate he ordered an address of
thanksgiving prepared for Washington in gratitude for his service
to the country. He also served on a committee with his cousin
Charles Carroll that prepared a similar letter of thanks to
Lafayette.

President Daniel Carroll and Charles Carroll tried to block
agency fees for Samuel Chase, a personal and political enemy
who represented Maryland in an attempt to recover Bank of
England stock after the Revolution. Despite their opposition the
Senate advanced 500 pounds to Chase to pay his costs and legal
fees.

Daniel Carroll joined the majority in the Senate against

granting the voting privilege to the non-jurors (Loyalists). He held it was premature to grant them the vote before the Treaty of Paris had been ratified and while British troops still occupied western forts. Charles Carroll supported the measure.

Daniel Carroll favored increased pay for judges "for they deserve more for their labors." He also supported measures to build a new prison at Annapolis and to found a college on the western shore to be designated as the University of Maryland.

In a touch that would be considered ecumenical, Carroll, the strong Catholic, supported an act that would provide relief for widows and children of the Protestant clergy. His cousin Charles Carroll openly opposed the measure.

But Daniel Carroll joined his cousin Charles Carroll and the aristocratic majority in the Maryland Senate in opposing paper money and the inflationary emission of bills of credit which had passed the lower House.

A movement to strengthen the Articles resulted in Virginia inviting the states to meet at Annapolis in September 1786. Only five states attended (Virginia, New York, Pennsylvania, New Jersey and Delaware) but the group adopted a motion to invite all the states to a meeting in Philadelphia the following spring for the purpose of "revising the federal system." Maryland failed to make the Annapolis meeting; Carroll explained to Madison the state Senate feared such a meeting would have a tendency to discredit the Congress. But Maryland agreed to send delegates to Philadelphia. Daniel Carroll was one of the Maryland delegation along with James McHenry, Daniel of St. Thomas Jennifer, John Francis Mercer, and Luther Martin.

Upon this appointment Carroll wrote to a friend, Michael O'Brien in Philadelphia, requesting that he find accommodations for him, a servant and two horses preferably near Germantown because it was "high, healthy and at a suitable distance."

As this appointment was neither wish'd for, or expected by me, and I have been detained from home all last winter, and six weeks this Spring, it will be some time before I can enter on the execution of this Trust. I dare not think of residing in Philadelphia during the Summer months. My health, thank God, is much better than it has been for several years past. Moderate (but constant dayly) exercise, temperance and attention, have in a great measure conquer'd my nervous complaints, without the aid of Medicine.

Carroll did not arrive in Philadelphia until July 9, 1787, 34 days after the Convention began. He was the fifty-fourth member to attend out of the fifty five who came at different intervals and was the fourth of the five Maryland delegates to present his credentials. He and Thomas Fitzsimons of Philadelphia were the only Catholics at the Convention. Carroll attended every session of the Convention from July 9th to September 15. He made twenty three speeches and twelve motions and served on three committees. He was the outstanding member of the Maryland delegation and also its most aristocratic. The most controversial member of the Maryland group was Luther Martin, a brilliant lawyer, an alcoholic and an ardent champion of states rights who opposed the Constitution on most key points. Carroll and Daniel of St. Thomas Jennifer usually supported the strong national government side with Martin and McHenry opposed. Mercer, the fifth member of the Maryland delegation, came late to the Convention and left early. Carroll at age 57 was one of the older members of the Convention, the eighth in seniority and the second oldest member from Maryland.

Carroll favored giving Congress the power of taxing directly but Martin and McHenry wanted to maintain the requisition system that had been such a disaster for the Articles. Martin introduced a motion that would continue the requisition system. It was defeated decisively although the Maryland vote was divided with Martin and McHenry for and Carroll and Daniel of St. Thomas Jennifer against.

The Convention adopted the proposal that all money bills

should originate in the House. Carroll opposed this and favored giving the power to either house. He explained his position on this issue to McHenry on the night of August 7 when the Maryland delegation met at his house to discuss the issues:

> That lodging in the house of representatives the sole right of raising and appropriating money upon which the Senate had only a negative, gave to that branch an inordinate power in the constitution, which must end in its destruction. That without equal powers they were not an equal check upon each other.

Pay for members of Congress divided the Maryland delegation. Luther Martin favored payment by the states, Carroll thought that a bad idea. Members of the Senate in particular who should have the national interest at heart could be starved by the state or conversely rewarded for their vote. Payment for members of the Congress should be by the national government, Carroll argued. That position prevailed when put to a vote 9-2.

In a committee on representation of which Madison was the Chairman, Carroll voted against the 3/5 clause. Surprising was his opposition to per capita voting by Senators. Here he joined Luther Martin in a rare union of the right and the left in casting the sole negative on this issue (9-1).

He supported Madison's amendment in committee that there should be a 2/3rds vote for expulsion of a member of Congress and a five year citizenship for members of the House of Representatives rather than the seven year requirement adopted. He opposed disqualifying members of Congress for having unsettled accounts as well as recognized debtors.

Carroll backed Gorham's resolution that the basis of representation in the House of Representatives be 30,000 per person rather than 40,000.

Three clauses in the Constitution that Carroll played a key role in promoting were 1) the ban on export taxes, 2) the equality of all ports under the commerce clause and 3) the permission for states to levy tonnage duties with the consent of Congress. All three provisions became part of Article 1, Section 9 of the Constitution.

Carroll played an active part in the debate on executive powers. Here the aristocrat showed distinct democratic tendencies. He preferred election of the chief executive "by the people" instead of state legislatures. This was defeated. He seconded a motion by James Wilson of Pennsylvania that "the executive be chosen every ... years ... Electors to be taken by lot from the national legislature who shall proceed immediately to the choice of the Executive and not separate until it be made." Finally, he seconded the motion of Gouverneur Morris that "the President shall be chosen by electors to be chosen by the People of the several states." This was defeated and the Maryland vote was in the negative.

He questioned whether a two-thirds vote was sufficient to override a veto, particularly as a quorum was a mere majority. Eight votes in the Senate would be sufficient to override a veto. He thought the matter ought to be postponed until the full extent of executive power was defined.

Carroll held that the central government should have the power to suppress rebellion and he thought every state ought to want it. But his colleague Luther Martin would leave the matter up to the states.

On the subject of public lands Carroll opposed any measure that would impede federal control. Hence he voted against the clause that required the consent of the state to its being divided. Apparently he feared that no new states would be created out of lands owned by states like Virginia and North Carolina that held huge territories west of the Mississippi and south of the Ohio. On this point he met strong opposition from an ally, James Wilson of Pennsylvania, who said "he knew of nothing that would give greater or juster alarm than the doctrine that a political society is to be torn asunder without its consent." Carroll's proposal was defeated 8-3 with Maryland joined by New Jersey and Delaware in support.

On August 31, all parts of the Constitution not acted upon were referred to a committee of eleven to which Carroll was appointed. He joined such distinguished Americans as James Madison, Rufus King, Gouverneur Morris, John Dickinson and Roger Sherman.

Carroll favored the consent of all the states to put the Constitution into effect. This was defeated in committee 10-1. Finally he proposed that the Constitution be sent to the states along with an address to the people. That, too, was voted down by a margin of 6-4.

On the 17th of September, 1787, the whole document was read to the members and signed. Carroll, Jennifer and McHenry affixed their signatures to the final draft. Carroll could return to Maryland satisfied that he had done all in his power to shape a constitution suited to the "exigencies of the Union."

Ratification of the Constitution

Although the Federalists, as supporters of the Constitution were now called, were strong in Maryland, the anti-Federalists put up a stiff fight. The latter were led by Samuel Chase, Luther Martin and John Francis Mercer. Chase, writing under the name of "Caution" in the *Maryland Journal*, denounced the Constitution and its supporters. Carroll answered him in the same newspaper under the pen-name of "Friend of the Constitution":

> It is neither extraordinary nor unexpected, that the Constitution offered to your consideration should meet with opposition ... I will confess indeed that I am not a blind admirer of this plan of government, and that there are some parts of it, which if my wish had prevailed, would certainly have been altered. But when I reflect how widely men differ in their opinions, and that every man ... has an equal

pretension to assert his own, I am satisfied that anything nearer to perfection could not have been accomplished. If there are errors, it should be remembered, that the seeds of reformation are sown in the work itself, and the concurrence of two-thirds of the Congress may, at any time, introduce alterations and amendments... Regarding it, then, in every point of view with a candid and disinterested mind, I am bold to assert that it is the best form of government which has ever been offered to the world.

The enemies of the Constitution in Maryland circulated a list of twenty Federalists whom they said favored a monarchy. Carroll's name was among them. He bitterly resented the imputation and, obviously distressed, wrote to his brother, John, the priest:

During a long course of Public Service, I have never before heard of an imputation being cast on my conduct. This is of a nature which would deservedly deprive me of the confidence of the Public, at least. My character I hold dear, and will maintain it against attempts to injure it. Where the blame is, I will not undertake to determine. I did not conceive it probable, that such a paper as is mentioned in Mr. McHenry's Letter of the 9th of Jany, could have been circulated among some of the deputies from Maryland without my privity, much less, that Mr. McHenry would furnish Mr. Martin with one with my name on it. Until lately I would not believe that my name was on the list.

The anti-Federalists tried to delay the ratification by offering a series of amendments but the Federalists insisted that the Constitution be voted up or down. They were taking no chances and they were determined to ratify it without delay or hearing. The ratifying convention met at Annapolis on April 21, 1788. Carroll kept Madison informed on the situation. He predicted that the Constitution would carry by a vote of 62-10 or even 63-11. When the vote was taken on April 26, the latter figure proved correct but Carroll's name is not on the list of those in favor as he was absent due to illness.

The United States Congress

The first election in Maryland for national office was a vigorously fought one with anti-Federalists promising to support the Constitution but insisting on a host of amendments if elected. The Federalists enjoyed a clean sweep winning all six Congressional seats, both Senators and the governorship. Daniel Carroll was a strong vote getter, finishing second with a total of 5819.

The First Congress met in New York City at Wall and Nassau streets with the House meeting on the first floor and the Senate on the second. Charles Carroll was the only Catholic in the Senate while Daniel Carroll, Thomas Fitzsimons and possibly Aedanus Burke of South Carolina were the Catholic representatives.

Daniel Carroll was appointed to the House-Senate committee on protocol to decide where the inaugural should be given, how the President should be addressed (John Adams suggested "His Highness the President of the United States and protector of their Liberties") and a host of other points of etiquette.

Some seventy amendments to the Constitution were suggested and Madison presented to the House twelve of these, ten of which were adopted. Carroll played a significant role in the debates on the First and Tenth amendments.

On August 15th Madison presented the rough draft of the First Amendment:

> The civil rights of none shall be abridged on account of religious beliefs or worship nor shall any national religion be established nor shall the full and equal rights of conscience in any manner or any pretext be infringed.

Carroll spoke from the bitter experience of the Catholics of Maryland on this point:

As the rights of conscience are in their nature of peculiar delicacy and will little bear the gentlest touch of governmental hand and as many sects have concurred in opinion that they are not well secured under the present constitution, he said he was much in favor of adopting the words. He thought it would tend more toward conciliating the minds of the people to the government than almost any other amendment he had heard proposed. He would not contend with gentlemen about phraseology... his object was to secure the substance in such a manner as to satisfy the wishes of the honest part of the community.

Given the history of the amendment and the status of religion today in American society an obscure member of the House, Peter Sylvester of New York, was a bit of a prophet when he expressed fear that the wording might suggest a tendency toward the abolition of all religion. Roger Sherman of Connecticut did not think the amendment necessary since Congress had no delegated power to establish religion; but Madison pointed out that Congress could pass laws that interfered with religion.

To the proposed Tenth amendment that read, "The powers not delegated to the United States by the Constitution nor prohibited by it to the States are reserved to the States respectively," Carroll suggested that there be added "or to the people." This was adopted and here again the aristocratic Carroll demonstrated his faith in the people.

Carroll was a protectionist. He supported the duty on molasses and favored a duty on glass to protect the burgeoning Maryland glass industry. However, he opposed an impost on spirits.

Imbued with the same spirit that inspired Washington's Farewell Address, Carroll offered an amendment to the act establishing the State Department "limiting the operations of the act under a hope that a time come when the United States would be disengaged from the necessity of supporting a Secretary of

Foreign Affairs." The geographical situation of the country "would be security against being drawn into the vortex of European politics."

Carroll ultimately supported the bargain that brought about the assumption of state debts in return for a southern capital but initially was skeptical of the Federal government's ability to take on such a heavy burden. He supported Philadelphia as a temporary capital since it was more centrally located than New York.

In case of the death or resignation of the President and Vice-President, Carroll favored filling the vacancy with the Secretary of State who would usually be at the seat of government. He cited the difficulties which arose in European countries when the regent was absent.

Daniel Carroll was convinced that the power to choose presidential electors was vested in the people by the Constitution and this he considered very sacred. Not all of his colleagues in the House agreed. Their confidence in the people was not unlimited. Carroll was showing democratic leanings surprising for one of his background.

Signer of the Catholic Address to Washington

Daniel Carroll was on a committee of Catholic gentlemen that sent a congratulatory letter to President Washington in March of 1790. Other members of the Committee were his brother John Carroll, the priest, Senator Charles Carroll of Carrollton, Representative Fitzsimons of Pennsylvania and Dominick Lynch, a wealthy merchant of New York. Purcell considers the praise in the letter "fulsome" and the tone almost "cringing as might be expected from a recently emancipated minority of about one percent of the total national population."

We have long been impatient to testify our joy, and

unbounded confidence on your being called, by an Unanimous Vote, to the first station of a country, in which the unanimity, could not have been obtained without the previous merit of unexampled services, of eminent wisdom and unblemished virtue. Our congratulations have not reached you sooner, because our scattered situation prevented our communications, and for collecting of those sentiments, which warmed every breath. But the delay has furnished us with the opportunity, not merely of presaging the happiness to be expected under your Administration, but of bearing testimony to that which we experience already. It is your peculiar talent, in war and in peace, to afford security to those who commit their protection into your hands. In war you shield them from their ravages of armed hostility; in peace, you establish public tranquility, by the justice and moderation not less than by the vigour of your government. By example as well as by vigilance, you extend the influence of laws on manners of our fellow-citizens. You encourage respect for religion; and inculcate by words and actions, that principle, on which the welfare of nations so much depends, that a superintending providence governs the events of the works, and watches over the conduct of men. Your exalted maxims, and unwaried attention to the moral and physical improvement of our country, have produced already the happiest effects. Under your administration, America is animated with zeal for the attainment and encouragement of useful literature. She improves her agriculture; extends her commerce; and acquires with foreign nations a dignity unknown to her before. From these events, in which none can feel a warmer interest than ourselves, we derive additional pleasure, by recollecting that you, Sir, have been the principle instrument to effect so rapid a change in our political situation. This prospect of national prosperity is peculiarly pleasing to us, on another account; because, whilst our country preserves her freedom and independence we shall have a well founded title to claim from her justice, the equal rights of citizenship, as the price of our blood spilt under your eyes, and of our common exertions for her defense, under your auspicious conduct — rights rendered more dear to us by the remembrance of former hardships. When we pray for the preservation of them, where they have been granted —

and expect the full extension of them from the justice of
those States, which still restrict them; when we solicit the
protection of heaven over our common country, we neither
omit, nor can omit recommending your preservation to the
singular care of Divine Providence; because we conceive
that no human means are so available to promote the
welfare of the United States, as the prolongation of your
health and life, in which are included the energy of your
example, the wisdom of your counsels, and the persuasive
eloquence of your virtues.

Washington received similar addresses from nearly every
major religious denomination in America and his answer to each
was to thank them for their support and express gratitude that
religious freedom in America protects all in their right to worship
God according to their lights. In his reply to the Catholics,
however, he added a paragraph that seemed directed to the great
non-Catholic majority:

As mankind becomes more liberal, they will be more apt to
allow, that all those who conduct themselves as worthy
members of the community, are equally entitled to the
protection of Civil Government. I hope ever to see America
among the foremost Nations in examples of Justice and
Liberality and I presume that our fellow citizens will not
forget the patriotic part, which you took in the
accomplishment of their Revolution, and the establishment
of their Government — or the important assistance, which
they received from a Nation in which the Roman Catholic
Faith is professed.

He closed with a warm touch:

I thank you, Gentlemen for the kind concern for me.
While my Life and Health shall continue, in what ever
situation I may be, it shall be my constant endeavor to justify
the favorable sentiments which you are pleased to express
of my conduct and may the members of your Society in
America, animated alone by the pure spirit of Christianity,
and still conducting themselves as the faithful subjects of our

free Government, enjoy every temporal and spiritual felicity.

Commission of the Federal City

While serving as a Representative in Congress Daniel Carroll was appointed by President Washington to serve as one of the commissioners to "survey the District of Territory for the permanent seat of the government of the United States." The other two commissioners were David Stuart of Virginia and Thomas Johnson of Maryland. Carroll waited until his term as Congressman expired before he took up his duties as Commissioner. It proved to be the most difficult public assignment of his career, involving endless meetings and interminable wrangling and wounded feelings. The problem was that two of the biggest landowners in the District of Columbia (Daniel Carroll of Duddington and Notley Young) were relatives of Daniel Carroll and felt the government was taking their land without just compensation. Then the Commissioners clashed with the brilliant architect Major Pierre Charles L'Enfant who drew up a Plan approved by Washington for the future capital complete with broad avenues, parks and public buildings. L'Enfant intended to operate independently of the Commission while the Commission insisted that he serve under its jurisdiction. The conflict with L'Enfant came to a head when it was learned that the manor house of Daniel Carroll of Duddington, a nephew of the Commissioner, was being built on land that was designed as an avenue in L'Enfant's plan. L'Enfant warned young Carroll that his structure was in the way and had to go, but Carroll refused to cooperate with the plan. In fact, he went to Annapolis to get an injunction and a warrant for the arrest of L'Enfant to save his house, but while he was gone, L'Enfant sent his crews in one night and tore the structure down. The Commissioners were furious and complained to Washington:

> We (Carroll, Johnson and Stuart) are sorry to be under the disagreeable necessity of mentioning to you an Occurrence which must wound your feelings. On our meeting here today, we were to our great astonishment informed that Major L'Enfant, without any Authority from us and without ever having submitted the matter to our consideration proceeded to demolish Mr. Carroll's house.

President Washington sent a stern warning to L'Enfant:

> In future I must strictly enjoin you to touch no man's property without his consent or the previous orders of the Commissioners. I wished you to be employed in the arrangements of the Federal City. I still wish it, but only on condition that you can conduct yourself in subordination to the authority of the commissioners, to whom by law the business is entrusted, and who stand between you and the President of the United States — to the laws of the land and to the rights of the citizens.

This effectively ended L'Enfant's usefulness but it was largely his plan for the nation's capital which was adopted. The conflict between the Commission and L'Enfant grew out of the fact that Washington had hired L'Enfant independently of the Commission which, however, had been given the power to survey and purchase the lands for the future capital.

Elizabeth Kite wrote sympathetically of L'Enfant but also with some feeling for the landowners who were losing their property to L'Enfant's dream city. "As for the avenues and streets, no compensation whatever was to be given, and for the ground taken for public buildings and parks only twenty-five pounds ... was to be allowed them the acre. Moreover from the beginning it was impossible that they should understand one another; L'Enfant in his enthusiasms, looked out, and saw the splendor of the city that was to be; they looked out, and saw beloved and familiar sites, tobacco fields, pastures, wood lots thrown into wretched and dire confusion and realized that their undisturbed life of affluence and ease was over, and only vague hopes held out as compensation."

Carroll resigned his position on May 2, 1795. "Enfeebled by age" and ill, he was the last of the original Commissioners to resign and had been the most active. His total compensation for four years work on the Commission was $1817.22.

Daniel Carroll took part in the laying of the cornerstone of the capital building on March 15, 1791. The services were conducted by the Masonic Lodge of that area and Carroll as a Mason and Commissioner participated in the service. Later in September 1793 he joined President Washington, a fellow Mason, in the dedication of another building. Apparently membership in the Masons on the part of Catholics was not unusual at this time. Carroll had been a Master Mason since 1781. However his brother John, the Bishop, refused to take part in the second ceremony although he did not forbid his brother to participate. Sister Virginia Geiger suggests that the papal prohibition against joining secret societies going back as early as 1738 was perhaps not generally known in the United States.

No doubt the headaches and heartaches of his role as Commissioner hastened his end for he died May 7th of 1796, within a year of resigning. The Maryland *Gazette* and Baltimore *Daily Advertiser* carried a brief notice:

> On Saturday Last May 7, died at Rock Creek, Daniel Carroll, Esq. a gentleman of unbounded philanthropy, and possessed of all the esteem of all who had the pleasure of his acquaintance.

And so he died obscurely and even the place of his burial is not known. For many years it was thought that it was at St. John's Church, Forest Glen, Maryland. But that site turns out to be that of his son Daniel who died in 1790. Some hold that he was buried in the courtyard of Holy Trinity Convent, Washington, D.C.

Bibliography

Geiger, Sr. Mary Virginia, SSND. "Daniel Carroll: A Framer of the Constitution." Unpublished Ph.D. dissertation, Catholic University of America, 1943.

Kite, Elizabeth. "The Washington Carrolls and Major L'Enfant." *Catholic Historical Review* (July 1929), pp. 125-142.

Purcell, Richard J. "Daniel Carroll: Framer of the Constitution." *Records of the American Catholic Historical Society* (June 1941), pp. 66-87.

3

Thomas Fitzsimons: Merchant-Statesman of the American Revolution (1741-1811)

DONALD J. D'ELIA

In late November 1794, Alexander Hamilton, Secretary of the Treasury of the United States, called at the home of one of Philadelphia's leading citizens. Thomas Fitzsimons, a respected and successful merchant, was a member of the national House of Representatives at the time and a stalwart Federalist.[1]

Not only Alexander Hamilton was asking for Fitzsimons' help on this occasion. President George Washington himself knew about the Secretary's mission, and agreed that Fitzsimons could do the job, if anyone could. Washington and Hamilton wanted the Federalist Congressman, with a reputation for integrity, to win support in the House of Representatives for the Executive's condemnation of so-called "Democratic societies" that were, especially in western Pennsylvania, "deceiving and inflaming the ignorant and the weak" and threatening the Union.[2]

---

[1] Alexander Hamilton to Thomas Fitzsimons, November 27, 1794, Harold C. Syrett, ed., *The Papers of Alexander Hamilton*, 26 vols (New York: Columbia University Press, 1961-1979), *17*, pp. 394-395 and nn. Hereafter referred to as *PAH*.

[2] Quoted from Fitzsimons' speech in the House debates, ibid., 395n.

Why did the "Father of his Country" and his Federalist administration turn to the Roman Catholic Thomas Fitzsimons in this crisis? If we examine Thomas Fitzsimons' life and career in the service of his country before that waning autumn day in 1794, we should be able to understand the confidence that his name inspired in Hamilton, Washington, and other leaders of the national administration.

Like Alexander Hamilton, with whom he was long associated in working to create a strong Federal Union, Thomas Fitzsimons was an immigrant. Not a great deal has been written about this devout Roman Catholic, and the details are not plentiful. But what we do know about the signer of the United States Constitution from Pennsylvania ranks him as an important Founding Father of the new nation.

As Professor Richard J. Purcell noted in an early brief study of Fitzsimons, although Catholics amounted at the time to less than one percent of the total white population, two of the fifty-five signers of the Constitution were Roman Catholics, Daniel Carroll of Maryland and Fitzsimons himself.[3] The Carroll family went back to the seventeenth century in America, but the Pennsylvanian was a relative newcomer, arriving here probably from County Wicklow, Ireland, around 1760.

Fitzsimons and Hamilton had something else in common, that gave both of them a hard, practical sense later about how to build a nation on a sound fiscal policy. Like his friend and confidant, Fitzsimons began his career at nineteen in a mercantile house, and he soon rose to wealth and prestige in the City of Brotherly Love. In 1761 or 1763 the young Irishman married a fellow Catholic, Catherine Meade, whose late father, Robert Meade, had left Ireland for the Barbados, made a fortune in the West Indian trade, and finally settled in the port City where his shipping and brokerage firm prospered. Catherine's

---

[3]Martin Griffin, *Thomas Fitzsimons* (Philadelphia, 1887); Richard J. Purcell, "Thomas Fitzsimons: Framer of the American Constitution," *Studies* (June 1938).

brother, George, took Fitzsimons into a partnership; and Fitzsimons was active in the business until hostilities with Britain began and he raised a company of militia which served in the Trenton campaign.[4]

In 1771 Fitzsimons joined with other Irishmen, Catholic and Protestant, to found the Friendly Sons of St. Patrick. The Catholic minority were parishioners at St. Joseph's, the first church of the ancient Faith established in a Colonial city. Stephen Moylan, the first president, was another Irish Catholic who was to distinguish himself as a patriot in the War for American Independence. William Penn's Quaker colony had, in general, been good to "papists": but during the French and Indian War the growing number of Catholics in Philadelphia was subjected to persecution.[5] As the conflict with Parliament took center stage in the Seventies, the penal laws and other restrictions against Catholics were relaxed. Moreover, the French were no longer seen as a threat, New France having been ceded to Britain by the Treaty of Paris.

Fitzsimons was soon in the ranks of the Philadelphians who supported Dr. Benjamin Franklin in his efforts to abolish the proprietary government which, after William Penn's death, had fallen under the incompetent administration of his sons. As for any loyalty to the British government, he could hardly be expected as an Irish Catholic to stand with the oppressor of his native people. When Parliament passed the Stamp Act in March 1765, setting duties on legal documents, tobacco, bonds, leases, deeds, and ship clearance papers in the Colonies, Fitzsimons banded together with other merchants in protesting the novelty of the tax.

The Stamp Act was designed like the earlier Sugar Act to raise revenue. But, Fitzsimons held, it was for revenue *only*: a

---

[4]Ibid., 274-277.

[5]James Hennesey, S.J., *American Catholics: A History of the Roman Catholic Community in the United States* (Oxford: Oxford University Press, 1981), p. 50.

direct internal tax and flagrantly unconstitutional because it lacked the consent of the American people. Prime Minister Grenville's "Stamps" were nothing more than taxation without representation, and illegitimate in Fitzsimons' Catholic perspective. "Revenues," St. Thomas Aquinas had written, "are a sort of pay regularly given to the rulers, that they may maintain justice."[6]

What made Grenville's New Imperial Policy even worse for Philadelphia was the business decline it was suffering in the mid-1760's. The end of the war with France and increasing loses to her merchants from the once profitable West Indian trade were causing widespread economic distress in North America's leading city. Hard money, always scarce in the Colonies, was now made even scarcer. Yet, Britain, contrary to all reason, was determined to impose new taxes on an already strained economy. This was an issue that could appeal to liberal merchants like Fitzsimons and mechanics alike. "Our tradesmen begin to grow clamorous, for want of employment," one citizen observed prophetically. "Our city is full of sailors who cannot procure berths, and who knows what the united resentments of these too numerous people may accomplish?"[7] But Thomas Fitzsimons was no demagogue. In the heady days to come he tried to draw upon the best resources of his Catholic inheritance, to reject mere expedient and always act upon principle.

Thousands of Philadelphians met in State House Yard in early October 1765 to protest the arrival of the *Royal Charlotte* from England with its cargo of stamps.[8] Flags were flown at half-mast and bells tolled as though mourning the death of liberty.

---

[6]*Summa Theologiae*, II-II, q. 62, a. 7.

[7]Benjamin Rush to Ebenezer Hazard, November 8, 1765, Lyman H. Butterfield, *Letters to Benjamin Rush*, 2 vols. (Princeton University Press, 1951), *I*, p. 18.

[8]Harry M. Tinkcom, "The Revolutionary City 1765-1783," in Russell F. Weigley, ed., *Philadelphia: A 300-Year History* (New York: W. W. Norton, 1982), p. 112 *et passim*.

Fitzsimons joined with others to prevent the landing of the hated stamps by adopting non-importation agreements to boycott British goods. The stamped paper was never unloaded. Instead, it was stored aboard the British warship, *Sardine*, in the harbor. The Stamp Act was repealed in March 1766. Parliament, however, on the very same day passed the Declaratory Act which asserted that it had the right to pass laws binding the Colonies "in all cases whatsoever." This, after all, was the very same body that — as every Catholic school boy knew — had removed the legitimate Catholic king, James II, from his throne and seated an upstart in his place. In Fitzsimons' view, Parliament had been a tyrant from its founding in the Glorious Revolution of 1688. The arrogant Declaratory Act was true to its arbitrary character, and he was not surprised.

The next year the supreme legislature of the British Empire levied new taxes in the Townshend Acts, which met the American objection to direct, internal taxes by imposing external duties on lead, glass, paper, tea and other articles coming into the Colonies. All the same, Fitzsimons saw through the stratagem and agreed with fellow Pennsylvanian, John Dickinson, who in his *Farmer's Letters* maintained that Britain's tax policy was still unconstitutional no matter how Parliament tried to mask its real intentions.

Once again the British lawgivers seemed to back down, removing all of the Townshend duties except for the tax on tea by 1770. It remained the symbol of Parliament's power to tax the Americans as it wished. A half million pounds of surplus tea from the East India Company, the beneficiary of the Tea Act of 1773, were shipped to the Colonies late that year. New York merchants refused to sell it; in Charleston, the tea was unloaded but stored and left unsold. Philadelphia merchants, like their counterparts elsewhere, feared that Britain was trying to monopolize all American business.

Fitzsimons was a leader in the opposition to the tea. One day after he and other Philadelphians learned to their delight of the Boston Tea Party, word was received that the tea ship, *Polly*, had arrived at Chester. There a delegation from Philadelphia hurriedly caught up with Captain Ayres, commanding, and dissuaded him from trying to unload the tea at his destination or even register his ship at the customs house.[9] "The baneful chests contain in them a slow poison in a political as well as a physical sense," Fitzsimons' Whig friend, Dr. Benjamin Rush, wrote in the *Pennsylvania Journal*. "They contain something worse than death — the seeds of SLAVERY."[10] In no small measure Thomas Fitzsimons must be credited with rallying the City's merchants to take their stand with liberty.

But Fitzsimons was not content simply to oppose the Tea Act in Pennsylvania. When Paul Revere, an organizer of the Boston Tea Party, came to town on May 19, 1774 with news of Parliament's closing down Boston Harbor until Massachusetts paid for the ruined tea, Fitzsimons began collecting money in the ship yards for the Bay Colony's relief. In recognition of his prominence as a merchant and opponent of Britain's New Imperial Policy, Fitzsimons was named to the Philadelphia committee of correspondence. This was an extra-legal group of citizens directing local resistance to the Crown, modelled on the first committee of correspondence organized in Boston by Samuel Adams in November of 1772.

The nineteen-member committee of correspondence, largely made up of merchants, coordinated with other patriot groups throughout the Colonies and provided revolutionary leadership in Pennsylvania. Once a mechanic himself, Fitzsimons excelled in working with the Sons of Liberty in order to bring together Philadelphia's often antagonistic classes in a plan of concerted action. As a result of his and other Whig merchants' efforts, by early June of 1774 the committee of correspondence could report to Samuel Adams in Boston that Philadelphia was

---

[9]Ibid., 118.
[10]October 20, 1773, Butterfield, *Rush Letters, 1*, p. 84.

solidly behind his proposal for a confederation of the Colonies in support of Massachusetts. "All ranks, with us," one member of the committee wrote to Adams, "agree to the Proposal of a general Congress previous to the fixing on any Plan of Reconciliation or Opposition."[11]

The First Continental Congress, including delegates from every colony but Georgia, met in Carpenter's Hall on September 5, and Thomas Fitzsimons was among them. The Irish Catholic, long a member of a minority denied the right to hold public office in Pennsylvania, now sat in that "august assembly" of men like Samuel and John Adams, Patrick Henry, Richard Henry Lee, Thomas Jefferson, and George Washington. Of the fifty-six delegates, more than one third had attended college and there were thirty lawyers or jurists. Fitzsimons was one of nine merchants. But as a man of affairs in the largest city in North America his outlook went far beyond the counting house.

His close friend Dr. Benjamin Rush, who himself later represented Pennsylvania in the Second Congress, was not alone in praising his humbly born friend of many years as worthy of the company of the great patriots of the times. "From an obscure mechanic he became not only one of the most enlightened and intelligent merchants in the United States," but what was more, "a correct English scholar and a man of extensive reading upon all subjects."[12]

After about a month of discussions on how to help Massachusetts by men "fearful, timid, and skittish" — as radical John Adams characterized the assembly — the Continental Association was finally approved on October 20. This was a non-importation, non-consumption, and non-exportation agreement, backed up by watchdog committees, to force Parliament to

---

[11]Quoted in Joseph E. Illick, *Colonial Pennsylvania: A History* (New York: Charles Scribner's Sons, 1976), p. 273.

[12]George W. Corner, ed., *The Autobiography of Benjamin Rush: His "Travels Through Life" together with his Commonplace Book for 1789-1813* (Princeton: Princeton University Press, 1948), p. 318.

reopen Boston Harbor and repeal the other Intolerable Acts. Many merchants were against sanctions, but not Fitzsimons who strongly endorsed them. Next year British imports to the Colonies dropped by 97%, although the losses were compensated by expanding European markets, and Parliament stood firm.

Meanwhile in the Boston area events were taking a more dramatic turn. Militia units were training on village greens and gathering munitions at Concord and other strategic centers. When in early April 1775 General Thomas Gage dispatched 800 grenadiers to seize the cache there and arrest Samuel Adams at the same time, a smaller group of minutemen clashed with the British force at Lexington and before it was over eight colonists were dead.

After the bloodshed at Lexington there was no turning back for Fitzsimons and other patriots. "America must be a colony or treated as an enemy," King George III was reported to have said. Committees of correspondence everywhere were soon transformed into committees of safety, paramilitary organizations like those in Massachusetts arming and training militia.

The mechanics of Philadelphia, rallying to the defense of their City and looking for men as determined as themselves, elected Fitzsimons to the committee of safety in August 1779. He not only offered his administrative expertise, but also raised a company of troops in Col. John Cadwallader's Pennsylvania militia and commanded it in the field later that year.

Back in Philadelphia in early 1777, the Irish Catholic patriot now turned his attention to the war effort in Pennsylvania, sitting on the Naval Board of the new Supreme Executive Council where he was responsible for constructing five ships to protect the approach to the city. Military supplies were also in short supply, especially saltpeter, powder, and lead, and Fitzsimons' mercantile company subscribed $5000 to equip the home militia.

Quaker merchants like Israel Pemberton, one of the wealthiest men of the day, disagreed with their Catholic friend's revolutionary position. True, Pemberton — the "King of the

Quakers," as he was called — had signed the non-importation agreement in 1765. But with the mounting violence directed against Great Britain, he and others declined to take the required oath of loyalty to the Commonwealth of Pennsylvania. John Adams, who like Fitzsimons was willing to risk personal popularity in the cause of justice, still confessed to a problem with the sect that was typical of many of his countrymen. They were a people "as dull as beetles," was the way he put it. "From these neither good is to be expected nor evil to be apprehended. They are a kind of neutral tribe, or the race of the insipids."[13] More extreme revolutionaries clamored for harsh punishments, saying Pemberton and his like were traitors to American freedom.

The venerable Quaker leader was to die as a result of his imprisonment in Virginia on the orders of the Executive Council, and two Philadelphia Friends were even hanged by vengeful patriots.[14] To his credit, Fitzsimons did what he could to restrain the wild passions of the multitude against the Quaker minority. Always mindful of his being an outsider himself because of his Catholicism, Fitzsimons feared the fickleness of crowds in times of public danger as much as any member of the Society of Friends. After all, Guy Fawkes Day, with its burning of the pope's effigy and threats to Catholics, was still an annual celebration in the Colonies, even though General Washington had banned it from the ranks of the Continental Army several years earlier.[15]

Fitzsimons was to remain an enemy of the Test Laws to the end. From 1776 to 1783 revolutionary state governments like that of Pennsylvania passed laws requiring repudiation of loyalty

---

[13]Quoted in Illick, p. 319.
[14]Ibid.
[15]John Tracy Ellis, ed., *Documents of American Catholic History*, 2 vols. (Chicago: Henry Regnery Co., 1967), *1*, p. 136; Sister Mary Augustina (Ray), B.V.M., *American Opinion of Roman Catholicism in the Eighteenth Century* (New York: Octagon Books, 1974), pp. 256-261.

to the British Crown. Loyalists were deported, excluded from public office and the professions, doubly and triply taxed, and their property confiscated. As a Catholic who was still subject to the infamous British Test Acts (they were not repealed until 1829), Fitzsimons and all men of good will were outraged. If the legislature "may banish at discretion all those whom particular circumstances render obnoxious, without hearing or trial," Alexander Hamilton summed up their position in classic terms, "no man can be safe, nor know when he may be the innocent victim of a prevailing faction. The name of liberty applied to such a government would be a mockery of common sense."[16]

Fitzsimons' defense of Tory Quakers, Germans, and, as it turned out in the event, fully a fourth of the population who refused the oath, was bound up with his opposition to the Pennsylvania Constitution of 1776. People who were against the Test Act of June 1777, required in the new constitution, usually wanted no part of the radically democratic state charter.[17] The loyalty oath, moreover, in effect kept critics of the constitution of 1776 out of public office and defeated any hope of reform.

Alone among the new state constitutions that of Pennsylvania did not establish a bicameral legislature. Nor did it provide for a governor with veto power. Instead an executive council of thirteen members was created. Finally, the Pennsylvania constitution of 1776 had a Council of Censors, popularly elected every seven years for a one year term, whose purpose was twofold: to determine the constitutionality of laws over the previous seven years, and to propose amendments to the constitution.[18] Somehow, Fitzsimons managed to be elected to the prestigious Council of Censors in October 1783.[19] He,

---

[16]*PAH, 3*, p. 485.

[17]Anne M. Ousterhout, *A State Divided: Opposition in Pennsylvania to the American Revolution* (New York: Greenwood Press, 1987), p. 162.

[18]Ibid., p. 151.

[19]Purcell, p. 280.

meanwhile, vowed to slay this "Beast without a head," as conservative William Hooper described the new government.[20]

Dr. Benjamin Rush, whose journals yield some precious information about his friend's role in the political controversy, wrote a pamphlet against the Test Law and took the lead in urging a drastic revision of the constitution. Rush, of an old Pennsylvania family, had none of the inhibitions that even educated and self-confident Catholics in the Revolution still experienced in speaking out on public issues.[21] A moderate Whig like Fitzsimons and a signer of the Declaration of Independence, Rush stood with the propertied and commercial classes who had, in the constitution, lost control to the more radical element among the mechanics, Scotch-Irish and German immigrants, and the farmers. What appealed to these democratic masses were, among other things, the widening of the suffrage and the belief that the new government would bring greater economic opportunities and relief from hard times. The constitution of 1776 had its defenders too among Revolutionary leaders like Dr. Benjamin Franklin and Thomas Paine, who approved of it in theory; and opportunistic merchants and professional men who welcomed a further erosion of the old social, political, and economic order.[22]

"I should be afraid," Rush wrote in his *Observations upon the Present Government of Pennsylvania* (1777), "to commit my property, liberty and life to a body of angels for one whole year. The Supreme Being alone is qualified to possess supreme power

---

[20]Quoted in Oscar T. Barck and Hugh T. Lefler, *Colonial America* (New York: The Macmillan Co., 1958), p. 579.

[21]Rush, *Considerations upon the Present Test-Law of Pennsylvania* (Philadelphia: Styner and Cist, 1784). Compare Fitzsimons and Charles Carroll of Carrollton, Thomas O'Brien Hanley, *Charles Carroll of Carrollton: The Making of a Revolutionary Gentleman* (Washington, D.C.: The Catholic University of America Press, 1970); and Fr. Hanley's essay in the present volume.

[22]Richard G. Miller, "The Federal City 1783-1800," in Weigley, p. 158.

over his creatures. It requires the wisdom and goodness of a Deity to control and direct it properly."[23] For the next twelve years he worked against what he called "our domestic tyranny" and "mob government."[24] And Rush, who was no friend to the claims of the ancient Faith, would have been surprised to learn that he agreed with St. Thomas Aquinas, that — in Rush's words — it was better to "live under the government of one man than of 72!"[25]

In the spring of 1789, Rush tells us, Fitzsimons spent an evening in his home with other prominent anti-constitutionalists planning the strategy which was to overturn the radical charter and restore political control to the moderates. By early September, and according to the plan devised that March evening, more than ten thousand citizens had signed petitions calling for a constitutional convention.[26]

At least two other Catholics of the small community of, maybe, 4000 Papists, George Meade and James White, had long been associated with Fitzsimons in opposing the Pennsylvania Constitution of 1776. Together they had founded the "Republican Society" as early as 1779, the society taking its name from the belief that government should be representative and — following Montesquieu — have separation and balance of the legislative, executive, and judicial powers.[27] The ranks of the Republican Society, it has been pointed out, as well as the anti-constitutionalists at large attracted mostly Anglicans, Quakers, Lutherans, and non-sectarians, leading one to believe that

---

[23]Quoted in D. J. D'Elia, "The Real Bicentennial: Notes on the Coninuous Quest for a Therapy of Order," *Faith & Reason 13*, No. 4 (1987), p. 359.
[24]Rush to Anthony Wayne, April 2, 1777, Butterfield, *1*, p. 137; ibid., May 19, 1777, 148.
[25]Ibid.
[26]Corner, p. 178; David F. Hawke, *Benjamin Rush, Revolutionary Gadfly* (Indianapolis: The Bobbs-Merrill Co., 1971), pp. 386-387.
[27]John Tracy Ellis, *Catholics in Colonial America* (Baltimore: Helicon, 1965), p. 398; Purcell, pp. 280-281.

Catholics too were numerous among the antagonists. On the
other side were mainly Scotch-Irish Presbyterians and other
Calvinists.[28]

In the raging controversy of the day, Fitzsimons and his
fellow Catholics were in the great tradition of the Church's
political thought, of St. Thomas Aquinas and medieval
Christendom, that government must be limited and conform to
the Natural Law or be resisted as tyrannical. They would have
agreed with Lord Acton's famous characterization of St. Thomas
as "the first Whig!"[29]

The Pennsylvania constitutionalists were soon in disarray,
especially as the new United States Constitution — which
Thomas Fitzsimons was to sign — weakened their extremist
position. By the autumn of 1790 the victory was won.
Pennsylvania at last had the republican government that
Fitzsimons wanted, a bicameral legislature and a single executive
with veto power.

Fitzsimons in these years of economic dislocation was too
much the realist to seek will-o-the-wisp solutions to the
Commonwealth's problems. There were plenty of other men,
however, who were not above demagoguery in offering the
people "bread and circuses" in the form of more worthless paper
currency. As a merchant with a keen business sense, a veteran of
years of experience in the brutal West Indian trade, Fitzsimons
held the line against further inflation. But he did more. In 1781
he and his partner, George Meade, subscribed $10,000 of stock in
the Bank of North America, the first modern bank in the United
States.

The nation's first bank was underwritten by a loan from
Catholic France and a son of Rome, Thomas Fitzsimons, was

---

[28]Ousterhout, p. 202.
[29]Quoted in Michael Curtis, *The Great Political Theories*, 2 vols.
(New York: Avon Books, 1961), *1*, p. 169; see Heinrich A. Rommen,
The State in Catholic Thought: A Treatise in Political Philosophy (St.
Louis: B. Herder Book Co., 1947), *passim*.

recognized along with Robert Morris, the superintendent of finance, as its co-founder. Capitalized at $400,000, a third of the money was, in fact, subscribed by twenty-seven members of the Friendly Sons of St. Patrick. Fitzsimons was to serve on the bank of North America's board of directors until 1803.[30]

The chartering of the Bank of North America by the Continental Congress marked the triumph after 1779 of economic, social, and political conservatism in Philadelphia. Men like Fitzsimons were now in the ascendancy after the revolutionary turmoil of the 70's, but the radical Whigs continued to attack the Bank as dangerous to the interests of the people. Meanwhile, the Bank of North America helped keep the patriot army in the field and staved off the financial disaster that had threatened the Articles of Confederation government before its founding.

While he was serving on the Bank's board of directors, Fitzsimons in 1782 was elected to the new Congress where his hard-money and other views about restoring public credit attracted the attention of Alexander Hamilton. The New Yorker had been considered for the post of superintendent of finance, which went instead to Robert Morris. But Hamilton's mission was to be even more important. As the nation's first secretary of the treasury he was to be the key figure in establishing the credit-worthiness of the United States, thus guaranteeing its very survival.

As they conferred together, which they did often, Fitzsimons, Morris, and Hamilton agreed on the need to fund the outstanding debt. Fitzsimons and Hamilton strongly backed Morris' program to overcome inflation and strengthen the central government, a program that turned on the states approving an impost. At the very least, money raised in this way could pay the interest on the debt owing to foreigners. Fitzsimons argued with great conviction then and later for the benefits of a protective

---

[30]Tinkcom, p. 147; Purcell, p. 278.

tariff. This was so much the case, that he is sometimes known as the "Father of Protectionism" in the United States. His younger colleague, Hamilton, would later prove his organizational genius and echo many of Fitzsimons' ideas in his important "Report on Manufactures (1791)" and other policy statements.

Before the "Impost of 1781" could go into effect, and the Confederation's debt could begin to be paid, all the states had to agree to give Congress the power to levy the import duties. Rhode Island refused to accept the proposed amendment to the Articles of Confederation. Fitzsimons, Hamilton, and James Madison, members of a special committee formed to deal with the matter, appealed to Governor William Greene of the defiant state to ratify. Fitzsimons warned against placing too much reliance on the impost as a source of revenue, but for now, he said, it was essential. The "increasing discontents of the army, the loud clamours of the public creditors" and the dwindling supplies of the government were so many "invincible arguments" for the necessity of the duties. "Calamities of the most menacing nature" were inevitable should Rhode Island persist in not accepting the plan to assure foreign investors that their loans to the United States were safe.[31]

Hamilton and Fitzsimons were always afterwards to have a close working relationship. Hamilton early saw the wisdom of relying upon his senior's influence with the business community in the nation's most important city. And it is not too much to say that Fitzsimons' role in implementing Hamilton's bold Federalist economic policies was critical to their success. They did not, as Federalists, agree on everything; and certainly Fitzsimons was no slavish follower of the man dubbed the "Little Lion" who made

---

[31]*PAH*, *3*, p. 210n; Clarence L. Ver Steeg, *Robert Morris: Revolutionary Financier* (New York: Octagon Books, 1972), pp. 130-131. For an example of Morris' great confidence and reliance upon Fitzsimons, see his diary for September 24, 1782 in E. James Ferguson, ed., *The Papers of Robert Morris, 1781-1784*, 6 vols. (Pittsburgh: University of Pittsburgh Press, 1975-), *6*, 423.

so much of his connection with Washington.

Fitzsimons and Hamilton were friends. But, along with other obstacles, Hamilton's "no popery" attitude kept them somewhat at a distance. Fitzsimons even helped find the secretary of the treasury a suitable residence when Hamilton moved to the new national capital in 1790. "I had wished for a Southern exposure," Hamilton wrote with an air of condescension, "but one cannot have all one wishes."[32] One looks in vain for any evidence of intimacy. On Fitzsimons' part, it is easy to infer that the older man was, as a Catholic and heir to the tradition of limited government, a little wary of Hamilton's well-known Machiavellianism.[33]

Hamilton has been called the "colossal genius of the new system" for his programs designed to win over the creditor and urban merchant classes to the new Federal government in 1790. Yet, as E. James Ferguson has argued, these programs were virtually identical to those Robert Morris — and his right-hand man, Thomas Fitzsimons — sought to implement in the 1780's. Fitzsimons' commitment to the program of hard money, high taxes, a national bank, and assumption of the states' war debts may be seen in his receiving the highest number of votes for the board of directors of the Bank of North America in 1781.[34]

If Fitzsimons had not been a Catholic, there is no doubt that his contributions to the founding of the United States would be much better recognized today. He should be placed in the company of Robert Morris and Alexander Hamilton as men of great organizational ability who performed the invaluable service of stabilizing the new nation's finances, establishing its credit, and encouraging the growth of domestic industry.

---

[32]*PAH*, 7, p. 5. For a discussion of Hamilton's anti-Catholicism in his early years, see Mary Augustina Ray, op. cit., p. 289. The present writer has treated his Caesarism in *The Spirits of '76: A Catholic Inquiry* (Front Royal: Christendom Press, 1983), ch. vi, pp. 87-114.

[33]Ibid., pp. 108-109.

[34]Ferguson, *Morris Papers 3*, p. 121.

But, lest we make the mistake of thinking that Thomas Fitzsimons was a mere bourgeois, a cold merchant and financier who played fast and loose with the lives of ordinary people, we need to look more closely at the man himself. Again, it must be said that the material that we have on his life is scanty. Still, we know from the evidence that we do possess that Fitzsimons was an overseer of the poor of Philadelphia, a benefactor of the Pennsylvania Hospital (the first in the British Colonies), a generous contributor to the Catholic churches of Philadelphia, and that he served as a trustee of the College of Philadelphia and helped raise funds for the new Catholic college at Georgetown. More than anyone else, he contributed to the cost of building St. Augustine's Church, which was served by Irish Augustinian priests from Dublin.[35]

In September 1781 Fitzsimons and his wife, Catherine, joined their pastor in trying to save the life of a young man who had been sentenced to be executed for deserting his army post. Their appeal for pardon to General Washington, through the good offices of Robert Morris, was granted, only to have the official letter tragically delayed and the young soldier executed before it arrived.[36] Fitzsimons also sought to relieve with supplies American soldiers held by the British in New York, but little seems to have come of this work of mercy either.[37]

A humanitarian himself, and like his friend a man above money-grubbing, Dr. Rush said it well when he described Fitzsimons as having only one, and at that, noble fault:

---

[35]Purcell, pp. 288-289. Fitzsimons also helped his friend Dr. Rush and others found the first Black church in the United States, the African Episcopal Church of St. Thomas, Butterfield, *1*, pp. 602-603n. He also helped save the historic Philadelphia synagogue Mikvah Israel when it was faced with bankruptcy.

[36]Morris to George Washington, September 9, 1781, Ferguson, *Morris Papers 2*, p. 201. The pastor was either Rev. Ferdinand Farmer (1720-1786) or Rev. Robert Molyneux, ibid., 201n.

[37]Ibid., *5*, p. 135.

> In private life he was truly amiable. Hundreds in various occupations owe their establishments in business to his advice and good offices. His Friendships were steady, sincere, and disinterested. He had firmness upon all occasions except one, and that was when his friends solicited favors from him. From his inability to resist the importunities, and even the sight of distress, he suffered a reverse of fortune in the evening of his life. Even in this situation his mind retained its native energy and his heart its native goodness, and hence it may be truly said in spite of all his many immense loses, he died rich in affection, esteem, and gratitude of all classes of his fellow citizens.[38]

Fitzsimons, Rush wrote John Adams, "died of a broken heart" from the ingratitude of friends who never repaid their loans to him. One of them was Robert Morris, who himself ended his days in a debtors' prison.[39] It is ironic that Morris, Fitzsimons, and Alexander Hamilton — the architects of the early Republic's economy — all died in financial difficulties.

It was almost inevitable that Thomas Fitzsimons should become a Federalist, a party given its very name by Hamilton and drawing its membership in Pennsylvania from the ranks of those who had opposed the unicameral government of 1776. In Congress he had first-hand experience of the awkward operations of the Confederation, especially its lack of taxing power. Indeed, he had personally known the frustrations of trying to convince Rhode Island that it must accept the Impost of 1781 for the benefit of the nation.

Something must be done about creditors' debts. The honor of the United States must be upheld; besides, if nothing were

---

[38]Corne., p. 318. Through Hamilton, Fitzsimons met and helped William Magee Seton, husband of St. Elizabeth Ann Seton, Purcell, p. 280.

[39]Rush to John Adams, September 4, 1811, Butterfield, 2, p. 1102; E. P. Oberholtzer, "Robert Morris," *Dictionary of American Biography* 7, p. 223.

done to pay creditors, foreign investors would look elsewhere and the United States would not be able to attract the capital that it needed for industrial growth and international respectability. Fitzsimons shared this vision of the American future with Morris, Hamilton, and all Federalists.

Not all of the nation's creditors were foreigners. Congress had promised the Continental army half pay on their demobilization once the War was over. Now that the end was in sight, some members of Congress were reneging on their pledge and the army was in an uproar.

Fitzsimons served on a Congressional committee to resolve the problem. Its members included Hamilton, James Madison, and Daniel Carroll, a Roman Catholic from Maryland who would join Fitzsimons four years later in signing the Federal Constitution. Hamilton and Madison, of course, were already developing some of the arguments they would use in *The Federalist* (1787-88) to win ratification of the new charter. These were men who knew that the problem of the army's arrears was just one aspect — if an important one — of the larger problem of the United States' credit-worthiness. Fitzsimons and Hamilton, especially, believed in the sanctity of contract, and that the honor of Congress must be above compromise.

In trying to resolve the problem of army pay, Hamilton proposed that the Continental Congress authorize taxes, including an impost. Another motion was then made in Congress to permit an impost whose revenues would be used exclusively to pay the officers and men of the Continental army. Hamilton objected, saying that while the end of the motion was meritorious, it failed to live up to the obligations of the United States to all creditors, foreign and domestic. Moreover, he insisted that, "The question was not merely how to do justice to the creditors, but *how to restore public credit.* (my italics)"[40]

The arrears were never paid; once again Congress had no

---

[40]Quoted in Miller, p. 93.

power to raise revenue except through voluntary contributions from the states. "If at the close of the war Congress had shown a proper spirit," Fitzsimons wrote later, "our affairs now must have worn a different aspect."[41] The army went home disgruntled, but there was no serious mutiny.

It became clearer and clearer as the decade of the 80's wore on that the earlier strategy of Morris, Hamilton, Fitzsimons, and other national-minded men, of reforming the Articles of Confederation, had failed. A new strategy must be adopted, that of creating a stronger central government, even if that meant by extra-constitutional means.

Hamilton, who could always count on his closeness to Washington, and Madison orchestrated the movement for a new constitution of the United States over the next few years. Daniel Carroll too became a Federalist, urging the ratification of the proposed charter in his home state with a series of articles in the *Maryland Journal*.[42]

To Hamilton, Fitzsimons, and other conservatives the situation of the country was fast becoming desperate. Imports and exports were down, as were farm wages. Money was as short as ever, creditors angry, and commercial and financial depression gripped the nation. Meanwhile, the increasing demands for money forced seven states to aggravate the problem by issuing $800,000 in paper currency, further alarming creditors.

Even as the Annapolis Convention met in September 1786 the worst fears of the conservatives seem to be realized. In Massachusetts a rebellion was taking place against the mercantile and financial creditors who dominated the government. The legislature refused to end the requirement that farmers pay their loans and taxes in specie rather than in the more available paper money. It would do nothing about the high land taxes, exorbitant

---

[41]Quoted in Purcell, p. 280.

[42]Ellis, ed., *Documents, 1*, pp. 157-159; Sister Mary V. Geiger, *Daniel Carroll: A Framer of the Constitution* (Washington, D.C.: The Catholic University Press, 1943).

legal costs, and court-ordered seizures of hundreds of farms in the western part of the state. Daniel Shays, a Revolutionary War officer, led one of the armed bands of farmers, and the rebellion has ever since been associated with his name. On August 31 the rebels closed courts in Northampton and in other towns to prevent seizures of farm properties. At Springfield, in January 1787, three citizens were killed by the Massachusetts militia.[43]

Shays Rebellion was crushed by February. But Fitzsimons and the conservatives now had what they had been looking for: the threat of civil war to unite the people behind the need for a more powerful government. Henry Knox, Secretary of War, branded the rebels haters of the rich who would stop at nothing. The Shaysites, it was said, were not above looking to Britain for aid against their American creditors. James Madison feared that social radicalism in Virginia would soon explode in a war of the classes. "Nothing but evil springs from this imaginary money," he wrote Thomas Jefferson.[44] There was trouble in New Hampshire with mobs, and New York called up the militia.

Hamilton's proposal at Annapolis for a spring meeting of the states to address the "exigencies of the Union" could not have come at a better time. He, Fitzsimons, and the other nationalists were no longer a small minority. In the winter of 1786-87, they were joined by southern planters and New England merchants frightened into action by Shays Rebellion and demanding protection of their interests by means of constitutional revision. Edward Rutledge of South Carolina believed that the rebels were dangerous levelers who would "stop little short of a distribution of property" and anarchy.[45] Theodore Sedgwick of Massachusetts, whose life was threatened

---

[43]Robert J. Taylor, *Western Massachusetts in the Revolution* (Providence, R.I.: Brown University Press, 1954), p. 160.

[44]Quoted in Ferguson, p. 249.

[45]Quoted in Szatmary, David P., *Shays' Rebellion: The Making of an Agrarian Insurrection* (Amherst, Mass.: University of Massachusetts Press, 1980), p. 124.

by the Shaysites, gave voice to the new consensus: "If we do not control events we shall be miserably controlled by them."[46] The Federalists had come into their own.

Once again, on May 13, 1787, Philadelphia went all out to welcome General Washington, this time as a delegate to the convention to revise the Articles of Confederation. His reaction to the "disorders" in Massachusetts, he was quick to explain, was his reason for being there. And he expected that every state legislature would send delegates.[47] The Light Horse Troop and other military units escorted the Virginian from Gray's Ferry into the city whose streets bore the names of trees, not famous men, because of its founder's horror of "man-worship." At the insistence of Mr. and Mrs. Robert Morris, the General stayed at their home on Market Street, the best in town. Both men were delegates to the Constitutional Convention and saw eye to eye on supporting American credit.[48]

Washington lost no time in presenting himself to Dr. Benjamin Franklin, the chief executive officer of Pennsylvania. He probably soon met Thomas Fitzsimons too and the other Pennsylvanians, for only two states had delegates in attendance at the opening session, May 14, in the State House.[49] The Irish Catholic seems to have been easily won over to Washington, whose paternal great-grandfather, a Royalist, had fled Oliver Cromwell's reign of terror and settled in Virginia. After Washington's election to be first President of the United States under the new Constitution, Fitzsimons was to congratulate him and — with other prominent Catholics — praise his "respect for religion" and fostering "by words and actions, that principle, on which the welfare of nations so much depends, that a

---

[46]Ibid., 122.

[47]Miller, "The Federal City," pp. 161-162.

[48]Carl Van Doren, *The Great Rehearsal: The Story of the Making and Ratifying of the Constitution of the United States* (New York: The Viking Press, 1948), pp. 2-3.

[49]Ibid., 9.

superintending providence governs the events of the world, and watches over the conduct of men."[50]

The Pennsylvania delegation, the largest at the Convention, was elected by the Assembly and consisted of Benjamin Franklin, James Wilson, Robert Morris, Thomas Mifflin, George Clymer, Jared Ingersoll, Gouverneur Morris, and Fitzsimons. William Pierce of Georgia, who arrived late, on the 31st, wrote in his famous character sketches of the delegates that "Mr. Fitzsimons is a merchant of considerable talents, and speaks very well I am told, in the legislature of Pennsylvania. He is about 40 years old."[51] Major Pierce could also have mentioned that Fitzsimons as a nationalist or Federalist was in the overwhelming majority at the Constitutional Convention, almost making inevitable the discarding of the old government and the adoption of a new charter.

Even before the delegates met, the issue of whether a strengthened Articles of Confederation government should be retained or a new "national" government devised, had been resolved. This was proved by the early acceptance of James Madison's Virginia Plan for a new national government as a basis for the Convention's deliberations. The Articles of Confederation was not to be amended but replaced. The new nationalism of Fitzsimons and his fellow-delegates was just too powerful for the localists to resist. The small-state delegates rallied for a while to the New Jersey Plan, which would have given Congress the power to regulate commerce and levy import duties, but once their influence was guaranteed in the senate of the new

---

[50]Quoted in Ellis, *Documents*, *1*, p. 170. Washington contributed to the building fund of St. Augustine's Roman Catholic Church in Philadelphia. Fitzsimons was the largest single contributor, Purcell, p. 288.

[51]Quoted in Arthur T. Prescott, ed., *Drafting the Federal Constitution: A Rearrangement of [James] Madison's Notes Giving Consecutive Developments of Provisions in the Constitution of the United States* (New York: Greenwood Press, 1968), p. 28.

government they too opted for nationalism as against confederation.

The real problem for the Convention was representation in the new central government, and Fitzsimons voted to maintain the freehold qualifications of the states. "Freeholders were the best guardians of liberty," the conventional wisdom of the day held. Liberty and property were inseparable, as the great John Locke had taught. Fitzsimons was against universal suffrage; for, as Gouverneur Morris, his fellow delegate from Pennsylvania, argued, "give the votes to people who have no property and they will sell them to the rich, who will be able to buy them."[52] It had nothing to do with aristocracy but with common sense. Besides, the people of the states were used to granting the suffrage to those citizens who were free and independent, and it should not be changed.

Clearly, Fitzsimons, Gouverneur Morris, Hamilton, and the other Federalists were still worried about Shays Rebellion and the debtor and leveling movements that stirred up the worst passions of men. They feared the "mob government" that had reared its ugly head in every part of the country and wanted to protect the citizens of the United States in the future against the tyranny that history showed always followed upon it. Yet, when the debate began on treaty-making in the new government, Fitzsimons showed that he was no party-line Federalist and that he could think for himself on the issues. He cast his vote for James Wilson's democratic — and subsequently lost — motion that would have given both houses, not just the senate, the power to ratify treaties with foreign governments.[53] This, after all, did not threaten the classical nexus of property and liberty.

No one at the Federal Convention was more of a "Rights of Man" advocate than George Mason of Virginia. He believed, as he said, that the lower house ought to be "the grand depository of

---

[52]Ibid., 214.
[53]Ibid., 460; Van Doren, p. 159.

the democratic principle of the government."[54] On September 14 he made a motion that "an account of the public expenditures should be annually published." Fitzsimons, while appreciating the principle of democratic openness, was too much the business executive to remain silent. "It is absolutely impossible to publish expenditures in the full extent of the term," he objected to Mason. A compromise requiring publication "from time to time" was the result.[55]

The vote on paper money was another matter altogether. Practically everyone agreed as "Honest Whigs" that private and public debts ought to be paid in real money and that state paper emissions were wrong. By the 1780's the total of these state emissions was some $209,524,776; and the Continental Congress, which could only look to state contributions, had itself emitted at least $226,200,000 in paper bills. While there is disagreement about the exact amount, between four hundred and five hundred million dollars in state and Continental bills had been issued, and the fact is that very little had been redeemed.[56] Every delegate was deeply embarrassed by the contemporary expression, "Not worth a Continental." Even the debtors at the Federal Convention, and their number was significant, moved quickly to deny the states the right to issue currency.

While Fitzsimons as a merchant-politician was understandably happy about this restriction on the states, he was far from pleased when the Convention voted down the motion that would have given the new government the power to tax exports. He was of the strong view that it should not only have that power but that of levying duties on imports too. Export taxes should be used in a

---

[54]Ibid., 41.

[55]Quoted in Prescott, p. 734.

[56]Janet A. Riesman, "Money, Credit, and Federalist Political Economy," Richard Beemann, et al, *Beyond Confederation: Origins of the Constitution and American National Identity* (Chapel Hill, N.C.: University of North Carolina Press, 1987), pp. 130-131nn.

future time.[57]

The most important decision at the Federal Convention, after that of replacing the Articles of Confederation itself, was how the new instrument of government should be ratified. How the "assembly of demigods," in Jefferson's phrase, would resolve this problem was not at all clear. Should the proposed constitution be submitted for ratification to the state legislatures or to state ratifying conventions? As he had before, Fitzsimons lined up with George Mason, author of Virginia's Declaration of Rights and a champion of the people. Only the "authority of the people," contended Mason, could ratify the new charter and that was not to be found in the state legislatures which local demagogues controlled. Hamilton favored ratification by the state legislatures in order, in his mind, to avoid any revolutionary radicalism and give some legality to the proposed constitution.[58]

Fitzsimons, who generally sat back and allowed Hamilton and the lawyer-delegates do the talking, broke his silence to point out the inconsistency of Hamilton's position. How could the Federal Convention, which had gone way beyond its authorization merely to amend the Articles of Confederation and had in effect invoked John Locke's right of revolution, now ask the state legislatures to approve its work? God had deposited political authority in the people, and they alone could ratify the proposed constitution.[59]

Fitzsimons' differences with Hamilton, here and elsewhere, give us a real insight into how the two Founding Fathers looked at the nature of government. The Catholic statesman drew back from Hamilton's manipulation of the people, as seen in his urging that the state legislatures and not the people ratify. Hamilton, at this time of his life, profoundly distrusted the people's ability to make the right choice. "Take mankind in general," he told the delegates at the Constitutional Convention:

---

[57]Van Doren, p. 150; Prescott, p. 720.
[58]Miller, pp. 181-182.
[59]Prescott, p. 152; Van Doren, pp. 136-138.

They are vicious, their passions may be operated upon. . . .
Take mankind as they are, and what are they governed by?
Their passions.[60]

Hamilton was in the tradition of Calvin, Machiavelli, Hobbes,
and Hume in his opinion of human nature; Fitzsimons stood with
St. Thomas Aquinas and the scholastics, Robert Cardinal
Bellarmine, and John Locke.

Government, Hamilton maintained, was too important to be
left to ordinary men, who were "reasoning rather than
reasonable."[61] His favorite political maxim was that "*every man
must be supposed a knave.*" (Hamilton's italics) More intelligent
men, men of self-discipline and *noblesse oblige*, the "few choice
spirits," must govern and somehow lead the masses of people to
see that the common good must prevail.[62]

Fitzsimons' theory of man came straight from Catholic
anthropology. His conception of man was biblical, i.e., the
human person was made in the image and likeness of God and
therefore rational and capable of self-government. But men were
not the source of authority in government, as, say, in Rousseau.
God was; yet the people could designate the form of government,
whether monarchic, aristocratic, or democratic. Any government
was acceptable, so long as it was subject to natural law — a
concept that Hamilton, following David Hume's philosophy, did
not emphasize at this time.[63] Since the people were entitled to
designate the form of government, Fitzsimons held in the
Scholastic tradition, they should elect delegates to ratifying
conventions. The Federal Convention agreed.

Thomas Fitzsimons explained his Catholic doctrine of

---

[60]Quoted in D'Elia, *The Spirits of '76*, p. 96.

[61]Ibid.

[62]Ibid., 95.

[63]See Miller, pp. 46-47. The present writer believes that Hamilton
returned to an acceptance of natural law near the end of his life, as he
will argue in a new biography in preparation.

government and his attitude toward the proposed United States Constitution in a speech before the legislature of Pennsylvania on September 29, 1787. Pennsylvania should "enter foremost into this new system of confederation, seeing the old is so dissolved or rotten as to be incapable of answering any good purpose whatsoever." It could not be said, he went on, that a confederation already existed, as some objected, since "if it does exist, it exists to no purpose, as it can answer no useful purpose; it cannot provide for the common defense, nor promote the general welfare."

What the delegates were constrained to do, Fitzsimons boldly announced, was to destroy the "greatest principle" of the already "decayed" Articles of Confederation, namely that of *"equal representation."*

> They found at an early period, that no good purpose could be effected by making such alterations, as were provided by the first articles of union. They also saw, that what alterations were necessary could not be ratified by the legislatures, as *they were incompetent to ordaining a form of government. They knew this belonged to the people only, and that the people only would be adequate to carry it into effect.* (my italics) What have Congress and the legislature to do with the proposed constitution? Nothing, Sir — they are but the mere vehicles to convey the information to the people.... the authority is with the people, and they will do it themselves; but there is a propriety in the legislatures, providing the mode by which it may be conducted in a decent and orderly manner.[64]

The "authority is with the people," WE THE PEOPLE, subject only to God and His law.

When Pennsylvania became the second state to ratify the Constitution on December 12, 1787 it was in no small way the personal achievement of the State's most distinguished Roman Catholic and merchant-statesman, Thomas Fitzsimons.

---

[64]Quoted in Ellis, *Documents, 1,* pp. 155-156.

Fitzsimons served in the new Congress for three terms (1789-1794), where on the Ways and Means Committee and in other capacities he helped bring to fruition the economic programs that he, Robert Morris, and Hamilton had struggled to introduce a decade before. Fisher Ames, a Federalist congressman from Massachusetts, wrote of Fitzsimons at the time that, "He is supposed to understand trade, and he assumes some weight in such matters. He is plausible though not overly civil; is artful, has a glaring eye, a down look, speaks low and with an apparent candor and coolness."[65] Most historians agree today that without the Hamiltonian programs that Fitzsimons advanced, the future of the United States would have been uncertain.

In Congress Fitzsimons became the acknowledged leader of the protectionist caucus, where he opposed the free-trade leanings of James Madison and the Southerners. He continued to be a close adviser to Hamilton, the Secretary of the Treasury, and a spokesman for the Washington Administration. In late 1789 Fitzsimons and fellow-Congressman, Daniel Carroll, drafted a letter to the new President in which they, John Carroll, Charles Carroll of Carrollton, and Dominick Lynch congratulated Washington on behalf of all Catholics and asked his further help in winning "equal rights of citizenship" for their counterparts.[66]

Fitzsimons was prominent too in seeking to locate the permanent capital of the United States in Pennsylvania. This campaign failed after good prospects when Hamilton offered Jefferson and Madison his famous compromise of June 1790, to have the capital on the Potomac in exchange for Southern acceptance of Hamilton's assumption plan, that is, payment of the states' Revolutionary War debts by the Federal government.[67]

---

[65]Quoted in Purcell, p. 285.

[66]Quoted in Ellis, *Documents, 1*, p. 170.

[67]E. James Ferguson, *The Power of the Purse: A History of American Public Finance, 1776-1790* (Chapel Hill: University of North Carolina Press, 1961), ch. xiv, pp. 306-325.

Fitzsimons agreed with Hamilton on the necessity of assumption; but he did have some problems — it seems — with the moral implications of not providing some compensation for the original holders of federal securities who had sold them to speculators for a fraction of what they were worth.[68]

Fitzsimons' political support of Hamilton and the Federalist Party in the 90's, while never calling in question his personal integrity, did not win him friends among the Anti-Federalists or Democratic-Republicans. These were men who, by Washington's second Administration, were forming around Jefferson and Madison to oppose what they saw as Hamilton's pro-British neutrality in the Anglo-French War, his funding and assumption plans, the establishment of the first Bank of the United States, and his overall favoritism to the urban merchant class at the expense of rural democracy. Nor did Fitzsimons' vigorous leadership in Congress on behalf of the Jay Treaty and the Administration's military action against the Whiskey Rebels endear him to the increasingly powerful Francophilic opposition. A conservative like Hamilton and Washington, if more articulate in his positions because of his Catholicism, he was willing to go with them to great lengths to stop the "French disease," the atheistic Jacobinism of the French Revolution, from spreading to America and poisoning the Judaeo-Christian well-springs of the nation he had helped found.

Jefferson and Madison early saw the key role Fitzsimons was playing in marshalling Federalist power in Congress. In 1794 they concentrated their efforts in an attempt to remove Hamilton's man in the House, and the Pennsylvania Catholic was defeated in his bid for another term. Madison lost no time in reporting to his fellow-Virginian that their man, pro-French and Anti-Federalist John Swanwick, had won decisively in

---

[68]Ibid., pp. 317-318n; Jacob E. Cooke, *Tench Coxe and the Early Republic* (Chapel Hill: University of North Carolina Press, 1978), pp. 142-143nn.

Philadelphia by capitalizing on anti-Hamilton sentiment.[69]

After his defeat in 1794 Thomas Fitzsimons held no public office except for sitting on the claims commission authorized by Jay's Treaty. As the new century dawned, his Federalist Party lost the Presidency to Thomas Jefferson. But even before then, intraparty strife between the followers of Hamilton and John Adams had weakened the ranks of the men who had once found unity in the movement to adopt the Constitution of 1787. President Washington himself seemed powerless to rally the elements of the old Federalist Party around a common standard.

Then, symbolically, George Washington died in the last month of the 18th century. It would not be long before Hamilton was gone too, a victim of a duel with the Democratic-Republican Aaron Burr in July 1804. The Federalist Party lingered on into the new century, but its day was over.

Thomas Fitzsimons, the last of the Catholic signers of the United States Constitution, died on August 26, 1811. Michael Egan, an Irish Franciscan priest and the first bishop of Philadelphia, was at his side.

Thomas Fitzsimons' life and thought have great meaning for his fellow-American Catholics today. He was, above all, devout in his Roman Catholic faith. Yet he was realistic about what must be done in his own historical situation to protect the *unum necessarium* for himself, his co-religionists, and his fellow-man.

In his career as a merchant-statesman he accepted the definition of politics as the art of the possible, never confusing this world with the next, the City of Man with the City of God. At the same time he never seems to have abandoned his idealism. As a businessman, and a good one, Thomas Fitzsimons followed his Saviour's counsel and did not put his trust in riches.

Thomas Fitzsimons was no narrow Federalist, but he did see

---

[69]Miller, "The Federal City," p. 202.

that Washington and Hamilton were right about what must be done to make the new nation viable. His positions at variance with those of Hamilton, discussed earlier, show that he was above what Washington called the "daemon of faction." Fitzsimons was a statesman, a great Catholic statesman, not a mere politician. His antagonism to French Jacobinism, with its hostility to altar and tradition in America and abroad, was in the spirit of Edmund Burke and counter-revolutionary in the best sense.

Pennsylvania's most distinguished Catholic was a man of no formal education, but of acute critical intelligence — the kind that G. K. Chesterton celebrated as the gift of the Church to her sons and daughters. And it was an intelligence always tempered by charity. The human person, Thomas Fitzsimons knew from his Roman Catholic faith, was made in the image and likeness of God; and accordingly, life must be cherished and protected — even the life of the obscure young man whom he tried in vain to save from the gallows in 1781.

Thomas Fitzsimons was, indeed, as his friend of 1776, Dr. Benjamin Rush, said, an uncommon man of great "energy" of mind and "native goodness" of heart. He "died rich in affection, esteem, and gratitude of all classes of his fellow citizens." "Few such men have lived and died."[70]

---

[70]Corner, p. 318.

4

Thomas Sim Lee: Revolutionary Era State Governor (1745-1819)

JAMES R. GASTON

I would like to thank Sister M. Virginia Geiger, of the College of Notre Dame (Baltimore, MD), for her kind permission to draw from her unpublished monograph on the life of Thomas Sim Lee. The monograph, which is untitled and undated (1950?), can be found at the Maryland State Archives, Hall of Records, in Annapolis. I would also like to thank the staff at the Maryland State Archives for their generous assistance.

Thomas Sim Lee was a Revolutionary patriot, and the second governor of the State of Maryland, and the founder of the well-known Lee family of Maryland. He is not a famous figure and the details of his public and especially private life are comparatively few. Nonetheless, the evidence at hand clearly reveals Thomas Sim Lee to be a man of impeccable character — a man whose adult conversion to Roman Catholicism appears as a very natural expression and the fruition of a virtuous life. The Latin motto, "Not unmindful of the future," long guided one of his heirs, and it justly summarizes the life of Thomas Sim Lee himself.

Thomas Sim Lee is a descendant of one of the oldest families in England. The name of Lee is of common origin with Legh, Lea, Leigh, Lege, and others, and all derive from the Saxon "lay" or "leah," meaning pasture or place. The Lee pedigree, first certified in 1569, extends over 750 years.

Lancelot Lee is recognized as the founder of the family. He originally came to England from France with William the Conqueror who, after the Battle of Hastings (1066), bestowed upon Lee a fine estate in Essex. The family position was further enhanced when Lionel Lee raised a company of gentlemen cavaliers at the request of Richard the Lion-Hearted and accompanied him on the Third Crusade in 1192. For gallant conduct at the siege of Acre, Lionel Lee was made the first Earl of Litchfield, and another estate, called "Ditchley," was bestowed upon the family.

Colonel Richard Lee of the house of Litchfield was the first of the Lee family to emigrate to America. He arrived in Virginia in 1641, during the reign of King Charles, as a secretary of the Colony of Virginia and one of the king's privy council. Colonel Lee also was a member of the House of Burgesses (1647), Chief Councillor and Secretary of State (1653), and he served on several commissions, notably one set up jointly by Virginia and Maryland. His first estate, established in 1642, consisted of 1000 acres in York County, Virginia. This tract of land became known as "Paradise."

Richard Lee, second son of Colonel Richard Lee, was born at Paradise in 1647. Owing to the early death of his older brother, John, he became heir to his father's large estate, titles and official position. Richard Lee also established an estate, called Mt. Pleasant, in Westmoreland County, Virginia. He died there in 1714. Six children survived him.

Philip Lee, the second son of Richard Lee, and the grandfather of Thomas Sim Lee, also was born at Paradise, in 1681. In 1700 he moved to Maryland and established a very extensive estate, known as "Blenheim," near the foot of South

Mountain in Prince George's County (now known as Frederick County). There are some indications that Colonel Richard Lee's original tract of land in Virginia (Paradise?) was so large that it actually extended into Maryland and formed the basis for "Blenheim."

In 1706 Philip Lee married Sarah Brooke, of Prince George's County, the daughter of Colonel Thomas Brooke of the long and distinguished line of Brookes from England. Philip Lee and Sarah Brooke had eight children. Sarah inherited from her father two of the most celebrated estates in Maryland, Dela Brooke and Brooke Place, and she left them to her younger son Arthur Lee, who was Thomas Sim Lee's uncle. Here one might note it is likely, though it is far from documented, that General Robert E. Lee, C.S.A., belonged to this family and his line appears traceable back through Francis, the second son of Philip Lee and Sarah Brooke. Philip Lee died at Blenheim in 1744.

Thomas Lee, the fourth son of Philip Lee, married Christiana Sim, daughter of Patrick Sim and Mary Brooke of Prince George's County, Maryland. They had two children, the future governor Thomas Sim Lee and Sarah Brooke Lee.

Thomas Sim Lee was born on October 29, 1745, either in Upper Marlboro, Prince George's County, where his father had a home, or, more likely, at his late grandfather's estate at Blenheim. Within a very few years both of his parents died leaving young Thomas and his sister as orphans. Their father, as his will provided (1749), divided his share of the family estate, Paradise, between the two children and he appointed as their guardians Major Joseph and Mary Sim.

Little is known about Thomas Sim Lee's childhood and early life. He was only four years old when his father died and therefore may have spent his boyhood years at his grandfather's estate at Blenheim. As for his education, he completed preparatory studies, and various unconfirmed accounts indicate that he also may have studied in Europe.

Lee most likely spent his young adult years, except for two years in Bath, England, in 1769 and 1770, in Upper Marlborough. During these years he frequently visited the Digges family at nearby "Melwood Park." Mary Digges, whom he married on October 27, 1771, was a member of this family and the only child of Ignatius Digges (?-1785), a wealthy Catholic landowner. Ignatius Digges' wife was Mary Darnell, the sister of Eleanor Darnell, who was the wife of Daniel Carroll, the signer of the Constitution of the United States.

The Digges were descendants of Sir Dudley Digges, the British Ambassador to Russia and member of Parliament, who perished in the struggle between Charles I and Parliament. His fourth son, Edward Digges, settled in York County, Virginia, in 1650. His son, William Digges, also had a son named William Digges, who was the father of Ignatius Digges.

Ignatius Digges had a brother, Thomas Digges, who entered the Society of Jesus and was ordained a priest in 1742. He taught philosophy at Liege, Flanders, and later became a missionary to the Susquehannock Indians in America. In 1773 he signed the Brief of Suppression, and in 1787 he signed the request calling for a diocesan bishop in the United States in preference to a vicar or a prefect apostolic. He died at Melwood Park in 1805 at the age of ninety-four.

The marriage of Mary Digges and Thomas Sim Lee did not occur without strong opposition from Ignatius Digges. The reason for his opposition was that the Digges were devout Catholics and Lee was a Protestant, an Anglican. This divisive issue presents the first and a very excellent opportunity to gain some insight into Lee's character.

Two extant letters from Thomas Sim Lee to Ignatius Digges reveal the crux of the matter. Each letter is quite brief and addresses the same subject. There is no documentation from the hand of Mary or Ignatius Digges. In both letters Lee fervently promised to abide by his future father-in-law's adamant wish that Lee educate the children as Catholics and allow them freely to practice their faith. Lee also promised the freedom of Catholic worship to any slaves his wife might bring to the marriage. This wish and promise were very significant in themselves and also for what they further reveal about the Digges family and Thomas Sim Lee.

First of all, concerning the Digges family, the letters convey Ignatius Digges' strong devotion to the Roman Catholic Faith and his steadfast determination to preserve this gift for his descendants and anyone else who wished it. Such commitment was hardly a surprise given the Digges' family history, Thomas Digges' vocation, and the fact that Mary Digges was the only child. Indeed, Ignatius Digges apparently took such a strong position on these matters that Lee twice felt compelled to write to Digges and fervently promise to abide by his wishes.

Ignatius Digges' strong opposition to the marriage also enhanced the likelihood that the Digges family was probably very learned and articulate concerning the Catholic Faith. As Thomas Digges' vocation indicates, and Ignatius Digges' first name suggests, members of this branch of the Digges family may very likely have been educated by, or perhaps they simply embraced the intellectual and spiritual qualities associated with, the great order of the Society of Jesus. Regardless, one fully expects such learned qualities in Thomas Digges who was a Jesuit priest, a professor of philosophy and a missionary, and he surely must have counseled and inspired the other members of the family. Of course, the Digges family was also in contact with and related to other influential and educated Catholics in Maryland such as the Carrolls.

As for Thomas Sim Lee, the content and tone of the letters likewise yield some insight regarding the character of the man. From the outset it is evident that Lee fully realized that his marriage to Mary Digges very likely would not have occurred without her father's consent. To this end, Lee made every effort to reassure Ignatius Digges that his wish concerning the practice of the Faith would be honored. But, even more important, Lee does not respond as one who simply sought to placate. On the contrary, Lee clearly displays a sound comprehension of and respect for Ignatius Digges' beliefs and wishes. In fact, Lee goes so far as even to commiserate with Digges' deep concern with life's essential matters, not the least of which is his responsibility for preserving the Faith for the future generations of his family.

The main point to make here is that the Digges family — by word and by deed — impressed upon Thomas Sim Lee their strong devotion to the Catholic Faith, while, at the same time, Lee's character was such that he was predisposed to receive it.

There is no written record of Ignatius or Mary Digges' response to Lee's letters, but, obviously, they all come to an agreement because Mary and Thomas were soon married. They named their first child Ignatius and he received his education with the Jesuits in Liege, Flanders. And approximately thirteen years later, sometime in 1784, Lee became a convert to the Roman Catholic Faith.

Thomas Sim Lee and his wife resided at Melwood Park for some years after their marriage. They later purchased a large estate, known as "Needwood," located about fifteen miles from Frederick Town in the Merryland Tract of Frederick County, Maryland. This estate originally consisted of 1500 acres to which more land was added. Lee was a planter. He grew tobacco, which was nearly the monopoly crop in Maryland and Virginia at that time, with the aid of about two hundred slaves. He sold the tobacco in England through his agent. Not much else is known about these early years except that Lee continued to hold his inherited position as clerk in Prince George's County Court which he assumed in 1767 at the age of twenty-two.

After the French and Indian War ended in 1763, the main

objective of British policy in the colonies became the establishment of a strong imperial organization. Parliament sought to finance this new authoritarian system by raising colonial revenue. But instead of advancing this goal, the various revenue acts, implemented during the course of more than a decade, slowly but surely united the colonists in militant grievance against the Empire.

With the Battle of Lexington in April of 1775, the tide of colonial defiance turned irreversibly against the British. Less than one month later, in May of 1775, news of the events in Lexington and Concord reached the delegates attending the Second Continental Congress in Philadelphia. The delegates responded by firmly declaring that although averse to immediate secession from Great Britain they were nevertheless determined to resist British arms and to remain free men.

From the beginning of the Revolution, Thomas Sim Lee espoused the cause of the colonies and moderately favored their armed opposition in their quarrel with the British. Yet he prudently refrained from taking any conspicuous part in the early phases of the controversy. For, as Lee knew, if the Americans failed the patriots risked the loss of property, fortune and probably their lives.

In July of 1775, shortly after the Battle of Lexington and the Congressional delegates' firm response, Lee publicly and fully committed himself to the struggle. During the Maryland Provincial Convention in Annapolis, a society called The Association of the Freemen of Maryland formed for the purpose of preparing for war. The Association promptly passed a resolution calling for the creation of an army to restrain and repel further attacks of the enemy. Thomas Sim Lee, who was present at the Convention as a representative of Prince George's County, was one of the signers of this resolution. Furthermore, he subsequently organized a local militia unit, the Lower Battalion of Militia in Prince George's County, and served as its Colonel.

Thomas Sim Lee began his political service to the State of

Maryland in 1777 during one of the most critical and interesting periods in the state's history. On March 26, 1777, Lee surrendered his commission and clerkship and accepted appointment and election to the Governor's Council. Lee was one of five councillors, three of which were necessary to constitute a board and carry on any state business. Lee's service was a courageous act, for Maryland was strongly divided over the war and many refused to sit on the Council.

Lee spent his tenure as Councillor serving Thomas Johnson, who was the first Governor of Maryland after the signing of the Declaration of Independence. Johnson, who also was from Prince George's County, was a very successful lawyer and a staunch patriot. Under his able leadership Maryland became one of the first states of the United States.

The details of Lee's service as Councillor are not known. However, during these two years he proved himself so competent that his associates considered him a likely candidate for the governorship. When Thomas Johnson's third consecutive, and by Maryland law final, term expired in November of 1779, Lee was nominated and elected to be his successor.

Thomas Sim Lee was elected the second Governor of Maryland on November 8, 1779, receiving the majority of votes from both houses of the state legislature and over twice as many votes as his opponent. And yet when Lee entered office he was not nearly so well known as his predecessor, had no previous outstanding public service except for membership on the council, and was only thirty-four years of age. Given such limited experience, Lee's election was quite an unexpected honor. And this achievement provides another opportunity to examine the character of this outstanding man.

Although Lee's election was unexpected it was nonetheless most timely and appropriate for two fundamental reasons. On the one hand, Lee's well-known social graces allowed him to perform the very special role the governor had to play during the first years of Maryland's existence. At this time the executive was, in many ways, much more the social than the governmental head of the state. In fact, the social demands of the office were so important that Governor Lee's election and subsequent success in part resulted from such public performance. In other words, as many of his contemporaries acknowledged, Lee possessed unusually well developed social talents, the exercise of which continued to add to his popularity and success throughout his life.

On the other hand, it was Lee's intellectual and moral virtues — not his social skills, as admirable as they may have been — that constituted his character and truly earned him such a solid vote of confidence in such an important election. Governor Thomas Johnson no doubt deserves recognition for initially collecting money and supplies, encouraging enlistments, and supplying officers at the outset of the Revolutionary War. But by the time of Lee's election in 1779 the first flush of patriotic enthusiasm was long past. And Lee's associates, clearly aware of the gravity of their situation, and recognizing the urgent need to secure a dedicated and able leader, turned to Thomas Sim Lee.

In other words, during such trying times few can afford to mistake propriety for principle. And Maryland was exceedingly fortunate to be able to call upon a man who possessed both qualities. Henceforth, it was Governor Thomas Sim Lee who bore the responsibility and successfully continued the important work of defending the state, and through it, the nation.

Lee served as governor for three consecutive one year terms, from 1779 to 1782, twice enjoying unanimous reelection. During Lee's tenure, which spans the remaining years of the War, his most difficult and important challenges were those which repeatedly presented themselves throughout the struggle. Two major factors influenced these challenges.

First, the Articles of Confederation gave the Continental Congress responsibilities but no real power. Congress could only request, persuade or cajole the states, and it was helpless if defied. Furthermore, Congress had no income or taxing power. Its successes depended solely on the working of public opinion. In this respect, leaders at the state level, such as Governor Lee, likewise had to persuade their legislative bodies, and citizens, to act in ways conducive to the war effort. This was by no means an easy task given the burdens of war and especially the division of loyalties. One can see why Lee's social talents were so important.

The second major factor influencing Lee's actions was the geography of Maryland. After the battle at Monmouth, New Jersey, in 1778, the British shifted their base of operations to the South, to the Carolinas, with the hope that a new tide of success would surge northward. This shift placed Maryland at the geographic midpoint of the conflict. In addition, British superiority on the sea compelled the colonies to move men and goods by land and river. The most expeditious north-south route ran right down Maryland's Elk River, to the Chesapeake Bay, and then on to Baltimore, Annapolis and the Virginia coast. Time and again, with little warning, Congress and General Washington called upon Lee to arrange for the transportation of men, material and messages. During the eighteenth century, in the middle of a war, such a task was very demanding.

Of all the recurring challenges Governor Lee had to face, and the one to which he exerted every influence, aid to the army was clearly the most crucial. In fact, one of Governor Lee's first official acts, in response to a desperate call for help from General Washington, was to issue a proclamation on December 29, 1779, calling for the collection of food for the starving soldiers. Immediately after this, in order to cooperate more fully with Congress and General Washington, Governor Lee organized a group of dependable laymen, and designated commissaries in several counties, for the purpose of rapidly securing and transporting supplies for the aid of the army.

The soldiers' welfare also was close to the heart of the Governor's wife. Mary Digges Lee, with a group of women, gathered supplies of shirts and socks for the soldiers. General Washington wrote to them in order "to express the high sense I entertain of the patriotic exertions of the ladies of Maryland in favor of the army."

Governor Lee faced a number of other important challenges aside from supplying aid to the army. Only the most important of these will be mentioned here. Maryland's ratification of the Articles of Confederation was the foremost issue because the question of national political unity was such a divisive matter. Maryland finally agreed to sign the Articles on March 1, 1781.

Governor Lee's other wartime challenges included in no particular order: meeting the state quotas for enlistments; pacifying the French, and her ally Spain, by supplying them with provisions (Maryland's extensive Chesapeake coastline offered the French fleet one of the few havens against British naval attack); addressing the London Bank Stock Company problem and the related thorny temptation to confiscate British property in lieu of the Company's release and payment of funds; and, resolving the harassing difficulty of a weak currency and an exhausted state treasury that made the payment of debts and salaries, public and private, difficult if not impossible.

The surrender of Cornwallis at Yorktown on October 19, 1781, signalled the defeat of the British. General Washington immediately wrote to Governor Lee and expressed his thanks for Maryland's assistance. "My present engagements," he wrote, "will not allow me to add more than my congratulation on this happy event, and to express the high sense of the powerful Aid which I have derived from the State of Maryland, in complying with every request to the Executive of it." As others note, this high praise by Washington more than entitles Thomas Sim Lee to recognition as one of the outstanding leaders of the Revolutionary War.

The tenure of Governor Lee's gubernatorial office came to an end in November 22, 1782. Both Houses of the Maryland

Legislature recognized his distinguished service in the following address:

> The faithful execution of the trust reposed in you as first magistrate of the state, together with your genteel and polite deportment towards all ranks, have given general satisfaction, and justly claim our warmest acknowledgements.
>
> Your close attention to the public welfare, and your firm unshaken conduct in the time of greatest danger, are proofs that the confidence of your country has not been misplaced; and your strict regard to the requisitions of congress and of the commander-in-chief, and the polite treatment of the officers of His Most Christian Majesty, has done honour to the state. Accept Sir, this public testimony of our approbation, and our sincerest thanks for the zeal, activity and firmness, with which you have so faithfully discharged the duties of your station.

After relinquishing the gubernatorial office, Thomas Sim Lee took up residence at Needwood Forest. But his life during the next years was not to be one of complete privacy and withdrawal from the affairs of state. A scant four days later, on November 27, 1782, Lee was elected to be a delegate from Maryland to the Continental Congress. The other delegates from the state were Daniel Carroll, William Helmsley, and Edward Giles. They appeared at the various Congressional sessions in March, April and July of 1783.

After serving as a Congressional delegate, Lee next became involved with the Potomac Company. For years a state of conflict existed between Maryland and Virginia concerning navigation of the Potomac River. In May of 1784, George Washington called a meeting at Alexandria, Virginia, for the purpose of settling these disputes. The meeting resulted in the formation of the Potomac Company and a plan to establish a water route to the Ohio River and West. Washington was elected president of the Company and Thomas Sim Lee served as one of its directors. At first the company influenced only the two states, but some maintain the Potomac Company annual meeting in 1785 exerted a powerful influence in producing a continental outlook on affairs that led to the adoption of the Constitution.

The Articles of Confederation, which had been a source of concern to Lee during his terms as governor, once again demanded his attention. The Maryland legislature, after having refused the year before to send a delegation to the Annapolis convention, finally acceded to the request to send delegates to the Constitutional Convention meeting in Philadelphia in May of 1787. Thomas Sim Lee was nominated as one of ten delegates, but he declined the offer. Nevertheless, he did serve as a member of the Maryland Convention that was called, in April of 1788, to ratify the new Constitution. Further, at the state convention he was appointed to the committee which had the task of drafting any necessary amendments and alterations. Lee strongly supported the adoption of the new Constitution, and he proved himself to be a strong Federalist, a characteristic he always maintained.

Lee did not hold any public office again until April 3, 1792 when, following the death of Governor George Plater, he was chosen to succeed him. Lee's first order of business was an act concerning education. During his previous term, in 1792, Lee supported the renaming of a small Maryland college in honor of George Washington. The present act provided for the establishment of the University of Maryland.

The so-called "Whiskey Rebellion" was the only other event occurring during the remainder of Lee's second tenure that is worthy of mention. In 1794, residents in portions of Pennsylvania and Maryland refused to provide the federal government with the required revenues from the distillers of domestic alcohol. The insurrection became a rebellion, and Lee, at Washington's request, helped in suppressing the revolt and once again asserting the federal government's authority.

In November of 1794, at the conclusion of his fifth term and second tenure as Governor, the state legislative body asked Lee to represent Maryland in the United States Senate, but he declined the offer. Shortly after this, Lee established a winter home in Georgetown. His home became one of the chief centers for gatherings of the Federalist Party, an organization he heartily endorsed. In subsequent years, especially after the District of Columbia was selected as the capital, Lee successfully speculated in Georgetown properties.

In 1798, Lee was unanimously chosen governor for an unprecedented third administration, but he likewise declined this offer. Thomas Sim Lee's political career had drawn to an end.

After leaving public office Lee focused his attention on his own domestic affairs. In 1798 he began to divide and sell portions of his splendid estate, Forest of Needwood, on the Merryland tract. The estate now stretched for nearly twenty-seven hundred acres, eighteen hundred of which were woodland. In 1802 he offered thirteen hundred acres in tracts for public sale.

There is no record of Thomas Sim Lee's later days other than that he was interested in agriculture and stock raising, and became a well-known judge of fleece and sheep. He also spent the remainder of his life in the improving of his estate. One also presumes that his interest in the state and nation did not cease when he withdrew from public life.

Thomas Sim Lee died at his home at Needwood on November 9, 1819, at the age of seventy-five. His obituary notes that:

> Mr. Lee bore a conspicuous part in the arduous struggle for independence... In Mr. Lee were happily combined great strength of understanding, with a sprightly imagination which made him as respected for his talents as he was admired and beloved for his social and friendly disposition.

His will, dated November 6, 1819, opens as follows:

> In the Name of God, Amen. I, Thomas Sim Lee of Frederick County, Maryland being at present in full possession of my memory and understanding, but being infirm in health and considering the uncertainty of life and the certainty of death do hereby make, publish and declare this my last will and testament, . . .

Lee willed one thousand dollars for the erection of a Roman Catholic Church, St. Mary's Church at Petersville, Maryland, in memory of his wife, Mary Digges Lee. He also devised an additional thousand dollars for the support of the church, and a legacy of one hundred dollars to be distributed among the poor of the vicinity. Slaves that were not willed to his heirs received their freedom.

Posterity is forced to draw its own conclusions concerning the personal appearance of Thomas Sim Lee, for he would not consent to a portrait. Accounts have him as a handsome man, six and a third feet high, and that every inch of him is "magnificently proportioned." He was originally buried in a private cemetery at "Melwood," but he was later reinterred in the Mount Carmel Roman Catholic Cemetery near Upper Marlboro.

Bibliography

Buchholz, H.E.. *Governors of Maryland*. Baltimore, 1908.
Geiger, Sr. M. Virginia. Unpublished and untitled monograph on Thomas Sim Lee (circa 1950), available at the Maryland State Archives, Hall of Records.

5

William Gaston: Ante-Bellum Southern Catholic Conservative (1778-1844)

DAVID M. ROONEY

The religious climate in North Carolina in the last quarter of the eighteenth century hardly made that state fertile ground for the emergence of a prominent Catholic statesman. Bishop John England of Charleston, writing the first account of Catholicity in the Carolinas and Georgia in 1832, observed that, excepting in some of the larger towns, many isolated practitioners of the Faith were so circumspect that they were often acquainted for the first time with a near neighbor's Catholicism by the bishop on his missionary tours, there being no priests and no churches around which to congregate. Going back further, he states that at the time of the Declaration of Independence:

> It might be said that there was scarcely one member of our Church in what is now the diocese of Charleston: still later, the tenets of that Church were scarcely known; the most strange notions were entertained respecting the doctrines and practices of Roman Catholics, and the greatest obstacles presented themselves to the introduction of their religion.

North Carolina was then, as it still is today, virtually the most Protestant region in North America. Indeed it should come as no surprise that in the 1776 constitution the colonists stipulated in Section XXXII that "No person who shall deny... the truths of the Protestant religion,... shall be capable of holding any Office or Place of Trust or Profit in the civil Department within this State." That discriminatory language, which the Federal Constitution's First Amendment of 1791 did not override, was not modified until 1835, with the assistance of the subject of this essay. Since Catholics were so few in number, the proscription of their participation in the highest state offices was not considered a matter of much significance. Of course, North Carolina's Protestants, like their New England brethren, had been fed a steady diet of English anti-Catholic propaganda as colonists, and were naturally ill-disposed to seeing Romish intriguers wrest from them their liberties by taking the reins of government and imposing Catholicism on unwilling citizens. Their fears were especially heightened by the 1774 Quebec Act, in which the British government granted freedom for Canada's Catholics to practice their religion unmolested. James Iredell, a noted North Carolina judge, denounced the act for protecting a church "persecuting in its principles, and horrid in its influence on the morals of mankind."

Oddly enough, there is some evidence that the state's representative at the Continental Congress, Dr. Thomas Burke, who also had a hand in writing the state constitution, was himself a Catholic, though never a very demonstrative one. He later was elected to the state assembly and then to the governorship in 1781, at a time when the British were occupying some of the state's coastal towns. In fact he was briefly held prisoner by the British late that year until his escape allowed him to return to his duties as governor.

Another victim of those British encroachments was not so fortunate. Dr. Alexander Gaston was a physician in the town of New Bern, which at that time was one of North Carolina's larger cities with a population of around 600. A descendant of

Huguenot immigrants, he was a well-to-do plantation owner who had cast his lot with the uprising against the British, serving on the New Bern Committee of Safety and occasionally as a Captain of Militia. When an advance party of British soldiers rowed up the Neuse River toward the town, they espied Dr. Gaston boarding a light scow to take his family to safety across the river to his plantations eight or ten miles away. Without giving him an opportunity to surrender, he was shot and killed in front of his wife. Mrs. Gaston, an English Catholic, was thus widowed at 26 and left to rear their two surviving children, one of whom was William, born in 1778. An early memoir of her, though cast in stilted prose, nevertheless gives a picture of a most devout woman:

> She survived the husband of her youth thirty-one years, in which time she never made a visit save to the suffering poor, yet her life, though secluded, was not one of inactivity. Her attendance on the sick and indigent was unwearied ... A room in her house was used as a Catholic place of worship, whenever a priest visited that section of the State. She was to be found at all hours with her Bible or some other book of devotion in her hands; her thoughts were ever fixed on things above; while the fidelity with which her high mission and had been fulfilled was rewarded even in this world — the gratitude, love, and usefulness of her children forming the crowning joy and honor of a life devoted to good.

Despite a paucity of resources, Mrs. Gaston contrived to raise her children as Catholics, sending William to Philadelphia to study under a priest, and then enrolling him as the first student at Georgetown College in 1791. There Gaston showed early promise of a strong intellect, which continued when ill health forced him to transfer back to New Bern Academy. Finally he completed his studies at Princeton, graduating with highest honors in 1796. He also emerged from this bastion of Presbyterianism with his faith intact, no doubt heeding the admonition of his mother to maintain contacts "with your good

friends at Georgetown." He then studied law under the erudite
French Catholic legal scholar F. X. Martin, later the Chief Justice
of the Supreme Court of Louisiana, and was admitted to the bar
just prior to attaining his twentieth birthday. As his sister had
married a prominent lawyer, John Taylor, who was elected a
judge of the State Superior Court, Gaston inherited his law
practice and began establishing himself as one of the state's most
sought after barristers.

His earlymost cases were argued in the eastern court district
encompassing Wilmington and New Bern. Frequently all the
protagonists were close friends of his: his brother-in-law as
judge, old schoolmates or teachers opposing Gaston's clients.
Predictably, not all cases were decided in his favor. He was on
the losing side of an important property dispute when he
supported the claims to a vast region of North Carolina real
estate by British subjects, whose title to the land antedated the
War of Independence. And he lost a spectacular criminal case
despite a spirited defense of a lost cause, when his client was
hanged on one man's evidence for murdering a cabin boy at sea.

But he did win often, and he impressed his confrères as an
assiduous student of the law and a formidable orator. His most
recent biographer noted the four rules Gaston would require any
lawyer to observe:

> It was necessary to devote much time to study, knowledge
> being evanescent. He [the lawyer] must acquire a thorough
> knowledge of legal science, a facility in expressing thoughts
> clearly, correctly, and agreeably and so arrange them as to
> illustrate, convince, and persuade; he must give an
> unremitted attention to the interests of his clients and finally
> have an incorruptible integrity.

And late in his career, in an address to his alma mater, he
reflected on the value of the craft he practiced so diligently:

> The law deserves our obedience, for that alone can
> reconcile the jarring interests of all, secure each against the

rashness or malignity of others, and blend into one harmonious union the discordant materials of which society is composed. The law throws its broad shield over the rights and the interests of the humblest, the proudest, the poorest, and the wealthiest in the land. It fences around what every individual has already gained, and it ensures to him the enjoyment of whatever his industry may acquire. It saves the merchant against ruinous hazards, provides security for the wages of the mechanic and the labourer, and enables the husbandman to reap his harvests without fear of plunder. The sanctity of the marriage tie, the purity of virgin modesty, the leisure of the student, the repose of the aged, the enterprise of the active, the support of indigence, and the decencies of divine worship, are all under its guardian care. It makes every man's house his castle, and keeps watch and ward over his life, his name, his family, and his property. It travels with him by land and by sea; watches while he sleeps; and arrays in the defence of him and of his, the physical strength of the entire state.

In the meantime he had married, only to see his young wife die less than a year later, and he soon remarried, his second wife Hannah bearing three children. With a successful practice and a growing family, he turned his attention to politics, for although he won election to the State Senate for the first time in 1800, he became a more or less permanent member of legislative bodies only in 1807. All told he was to serve seven terms in the State Assembly and four in the State Senate, in addition to his congressional and judicial years upon which his fame chiefly rests.

Being a Federalist, he was a member of the minority, for Jeffersonian Republicans dominated the North Carolina delegations. National issues frequently intruded on the state legislative process, and Gaston was found urging his colleagues not to pay obsequious honor to Jefferson for edging the country closer to renewed conflict with England. In 1810 he was defeated by a rabid Republican in his first attempt at a U. S. Congressional seat. But when Jefferson's successor James Madison was led to declare war in June 1812, Gaston contested and won a seat in the House of Representatives as a Federalist member in the Thirteenth Congress, also known as the War Congress. The platform he ran on was decidedly anti-war, as he called the declaration of hostilities with England "an act of extravagance and rashness, astonishing and unaccountable." He went on to say:

> The difference between the United States and our enemy is now understood to be confined to a single point, the right of search for British sea-men. I will not as a man and, as a Christian, I dare not, yield my consent to shed blood or waste the treasure of my countrymen upon an abstract question of doubtful right. At whatever risque [sic] or cost, I am prepared to protect my country and every section of it from attack, but I am not disposed to aid it in schemes of foreign conquests.

This term and a succeeding one marked his only foray into national elective politics, but he quickly garnered attention in a body which also boasted Henry Clay, John Calhoun and Daniel Webster among its members. Clay and Calhoun, of course, were leaders of the War Hawks, while Gaston shared company with Webster and the other Federalists. He denounced the war as a thinly veiled excuse for invading and conquering Canada, and warned that "so fatal is war to the best interests of the human family that a tremendous responsibility always rests upon the nation that commences it." Addressing the pro-war insinuation that the Canadians had incited Western Indian tribes to attack first, he held:

> There is no evidence of this last charge. Over... the commencement of the Indian war, there hovers a mystery which ought to be dissipated, but which the government will not dispel. I have honestly sought for information. From private sources friendly to this war and connected with the Western feeling and interest, I learn the great cause is to be

found in our cupidity for their lands, and their jealousy and distrust of our superior intelligence and force.

On the floor of Congress, he further incurred the enmity of the prosecutors of the war by offering a rationale for British threats to charge with the crime of treason a band of Americans caught during an incursion into Canadian territory, on the grounds that they were former subjects of the empire themselves. Likewise he argued vociferously against a $25,000,000 loan bill Madison wanted passed to support the war effort, which was not proceeding very well. Gaston even offered an amendment (roundly defeated by the Republican majority) to repeal the embargo against British and French commercial shipping. Federalists in general suspected that Madison's justification for fighting Britain, *i.e.*, that country's belligerent treatment of American seamen, was either a ruse or sad evidence that the administration "has been the dupe of France," maneuvered by the wily Napoleon into making war on his greatest enemy. Indeed Gaston believed that were Britain to propose an armistice and cease assaulting Americans, Madison would rebuff their overtures because "at that moment, the Canada fever raged high, and the delirium of conquest was at its acme. In a few weeks the American flag was to wave triumphant on the ramparts of Quebec."

Gaston's feelings were shared, if more discreetly, by other Catholic Federalists outside the halls of Congress. Archbishop John Carroll, whose see city of Baltimore erupted in anti-war riots following the declaration of war, had earlier written to an English friend that "a majority of Congress seem to be infatuated with a blind predilection for France and an unconquerable hostility to England... Every day seems to bring us nearer to open hostility, in which we have everything to lose, and nothing to gain." Similar sentiments were given voice by the influential Philadelphia literary figure Robert Walsh. But at least one prominent Catholic blamed Federalist conservatism for the peril into which the nation had fallen, with British depredations in Washington, and barely averted in Baltimore. Matthew Carey, an Irish-born Philadelphia publisher, alleged treasonable motives on the part of Federalist opponents of the war:

> The safety, the welfare, the happiness of eight millions of people and their posterity, were jeopardized and exposed to ruin, in the unholy struggle. To embarrass, disgrace, and render odious and unpopular the men possessed of power, for the purpose of displacing them, and vaulting into the vacant seats, is a procedure, as ancient as government itself. And that it has been almost universally prevalent here, is incontrovertible.

Federalism, of which Gaston was a most eloquent exponent, was being belabored for factionalizing government, a charge they would heatedly deny. The very essence of Gaston's political philosophy, to the extent he could be said to have consciously formed one, was its exaltation of social cohesion, to be achieved by the dampening of party politics, much as he may have had to modify that tenet in practice in a highly polarized Congress. The spirit of faction had overwhelmed the country with Jeffersonian democracy, and threatened to divide the republic into camps of victors and of vanquished. Speaking against a resolution backed by Clay which would allow a Congressional majority to cut off debate and force a vote on a controverted issue, Gaston argued:

> No majority should be trusted with it. A majority never can be found who will use it discreetly. The day you make a man a slave, it has been said, you deprive him of half his virtue. The day you make him a despot you rob him of all. Human nature cannot endure unlimited power, and bodies of men are not more discreet in their tyranny than individual tyrants.

Gaston's political idols were Washington and Hamilton, and he had little time for Jefferson and Madison. When Madison first ran for President in 1808, Gaston subjected him to a searching comparison with the late founder of the country. Washington, though not possessed of Madison's intellectual endowments, had a "commanding and comprehensive mind" as well as "that invincible firmness of nerves, which marked him as one destined by his Creator to watch over the interests and to wield the strength of a nation." Madison, on the other hand, might "sacrifice the plain substantial interests of the nation to visionary schemes of fancied good, and often be perplexed with refined speculations."

During the war, Gaston's wife Hannah, already weakened with the impending arrival of their fourth child, had died tragically of fright amid reports that British troops were making their way once again toward New Bern. Within a few years, however, he married a third time, in the Georgetown chapel. But his new wife Eliza, was also physically frail, and after the birth of their second child in 1819, she too died. Thus for the third time Gaston became a widower, now with five surviving children ranging in age from twelve to but a few weeks. The eldest three were sent off to boarding school, his two daughters to the Emmitsburg nuns and his son to Mt. St. Mary's, and the youngest ones were cared for by his last wife's family in Washington.

When the Fourteenth Congress adjourned in 1816, the venue for Gaston's political interests shifted once more to his home state, and he had renewed his residency in New Bern. He himself left a description of a typical day spent at home during these years. "In my office every morning from sunrise till ten — at the Bank till one — a short solitary dinner — the whole of the afternoon engaged in reading and writing — I scarcely see a person except on business, and scarcely know what those around me are doing." One authority on his life notes that his reading interests were broad: "He read widely in law, history and biography, theology, economics, and literature, not only in English but also in Latin, Greek, and French, and his tenacious memory, carefully trained from boyhood, enabled him to command the services of these allies at will." That same authority, R. D. W. Connor, one time national archivist and conservator of Gaston's private papers, went on to describe his personality as follows: "His social instincts were highly developed. Handsome, genial, witty; brilliant in small talk as in learned discussion as the occasion required; his mind a storehouse of anecdote and wisdom drawn from wide reading and varied experience; considerate always of others, he found a welcome in any circle, irrespective of age or position, into which he chose to enter."

In 1818 he returned to the North Carolina State Senate, where he was instrumental in setting up its Supreme Court, to be composed of three judges, who would serve as the final statewide court of appeals, thereby streamlining the state's previously cumbersome judicial machinery. The first Chief Justice was his brother-in-law, the Superior Court Judge John Taylor. Afterward Gaston jealously guarded this court from frequent attempts by disgruntled legislators to dissolve it or to slash its members' salaries.

At home he began a friendship with the newly appointed Bishop John England of Charleston, who had arrived from Ireland to mould a dispirited and fractious flock into a functioning diocesan unit. At this time, there was not a single Catholic priest serving the people of North Carolina. In 1818 Gaston had been one among a group of petitioners to seek from Archbishop Marechal of Baltimore a full-time priest for New Bern. A priest from Norfolk, Virginia had visited the state a few times a year, most recently in November 1820, when Bishop England wrote to Gaston in May 1821 announcing an upcoming visit. What the public practice of the Faith in New Bern would encompass in Gaston's mature years can be gleaned from England's letter:

> My object is, in the first place, to afford to my flock an opportunity of receiving the Holy Sacraments of Penance, Eucharist, Confirmation & Baptism. Next, to organize them into congregations, so that even when there is no clergyman

they may assemble together on the Lord's day and have appropriate prayers read by some person whom I shall authorize for the purpose, & have instruction by means of proper books which shall be read, — & the Catechism taught to the ignorant... With respect to New Bern, I should be happy immediately to place a clergyman in charge of the congregation there and in North Washington, but I have met a variety of disappointments which will prevent my wish and yours being immediately gratified.

A treasury was set up to buy a plot to build a permanent church, and Gaston headed the subscription list with a donation of $700. Not until 1824, however, could a priest be appointed full time to minister to the New Bern Catholics, and only in 1838 could the entire state boast two resident priests.

After staying two weeks with the Gaston family, Bishop England continued his visitation northward, finding a solitary Catholic at Plymouth on the Roanoke River, some twenty or so indifferent souls in Edenton, and he then preached at a court house in Elizabeth before passing on to Virginia. The influence of Gaston can be inferred from a stop made in Raleigh during the bishop's return journey. He was met by Judge Taylor and granted the use of a Presbyterian church in which to preach in front of "a very large and respectable Congregation amongst whom were the Governor of the State and the Judges of the Supreme Court." Pleased with his reception he wrote afterward to Gaston:

I have preached in the Presbyterian church on every evening since my arrival, more in detail than in Newberne [sic], & taking notice of those points which you were kind enough to indicate, & for which I feel much obliged. I find the impression has been generally favourable... A beginning has been made here. I hope God will enable us to follow it up.

The 1824 Presidential elections saw Gaston initially supporting the candidacy of his old Congressional foe John

Calhoun, until the latter withdrew. Then he switched his allegiance, tepidly at first, to John Quincy Adams in preference to Andrew Jackson. Adams, elected by the House of Representatives, considered appointing Gaston Secretary of War, but was convinced otherwise by, among others, his Secretary of State, Henry Clay, who had also crossed verbal swords with the sharp-witted Carolinian. As the administration progressed, he became a more ardent supporter of Adams and delivered an address at a December 1827 convention casting doubt on Jackson's fitness for the presidency, while lauding Adams' qualifications. In a letter to a friend he referred to the administration as "the friends of order and civil government," while castigating Jackson and his allies as "the rowdies of the day who depend for their influence on appeals to the malignant passions of the vulgar and the prejudices of the ignorant."

In 1827 he returned again to the North Carolina House and exerted his oratorical skills defending the state's banks (he served as president of one of them) against the demagogic attacks of populist legislators who wanted them disbanded. Indeed, regardless of the forum in which he found himself, Gaston invariably took decided stands. Yet the reminiscences of a contemporary North Carolina politician, David Swain, suggest that by then he was suffering "sleepless hours" meditating on the difficulty of preserving one's integrity when engaging in such rancorous disputes, since:

> on a calm review of the course of his life, too many instances presented themselves when he convicted himself of having been influenced to an extent of which he had no suspicion at the moment, by other than purely patriotic considerations. In addition to this it had been his fate on repeated occasions to be loudly applauded for what in his own conscience he regarded as least praiseworthy, and to be bitterly reviled for what he considered to have been the purest and most discreet acts of his public life.

But soon an economic issue of portentous national

significance emerged into view, demanding a statesmanlike response. The high tariffs being enacted by Congress on finished goods were leaving the underdeveloped South at a particular disadvantage with respect to the North. South Carolina, with Senator (and ex-Vice President) John Calhoun as its voice, was so resentful of the imposition of the equivalent of taxes on their importation of goods that it developed a doctrine that states could nullify repugnant Federal statutes, unless overridden by three fourths of the states. William Gaston and a large majority in the North Carolina legislature rejected the South Carolina thesis as dangerous to the preservation of the Union. In a speech to the students of the University of North Carolina in 1832 he struck a familiar Federalist theme, warning of the dangers of factionalism inherent in the South Carolina nullification argument:

> Now has come a period dreaded by Washington ... As yet the sentiment so deeply planted in the hearts of the yeomanry that union is strength has not been uprooted. As yet they take pride in the United States. May God in his mercy forbid that I or you should live to see the day when this feeling shall be extinct.... But these feelings are weakened and in the end will be destroyed unless moderates frown on any attempt to alienate any portion of our country from the rest.

And privately he wrote of Calhoun:

> It is impossible however for any subtlety or sophistry to uphold a doctrine which involves such glaring and practical absurdities. What a pity that such a mind as his should be so warped from its rectitude by unholy passions.

The next year, after resisting attempts to convince him to allow his nomination to the State Supreme Court, Gaston finally relented, but in doing so had to face again the apparent illegality of a Catholic accepting such office according to Article XXXII of the State Constitution. The previous year he had discussed the issue with Thomas Ruffin, then a Justice and soon to be Chief Justice of the Court. Ruffin had written to him:

> I have much confidence in the conclusion I have long ago arrived at, that a Roman Catholic may lawfully, before God and Man, undertake to serve North Carolina to the best of his ability in any civil office according to his natural allegiance and his personal duty.... I am very decidedly persuaded, and have long been, that Roman Catholics cannot, without giving to the terms of the Constitution a latitude and force altogether unauthorized, be excluded from civil office.

The opinion of John Marshall, Chief Justice of the U.S. Supreme Court, was also solicited by Gaston. Marshall noted that the clause was insupportable because no one could be cited to state exactly what constituted "the truths of the Protestant Religion."

When the vacancy in the court arose in 1833, Gaston wrote to Ruffin that his scruples about holding office had been removed and that he would accept the nomination because of his esteem for the office, even though it would mean a sharp drop in income and enduring public criticism from "every miserable demagogue [who] feels that he has a right to enquire whether the work which a Judge does is worth what he is paid for it." He continued in a vein which shows how ill-inclined many legislators were to accept the concept of a Supreme Court:

> The bare discussion of such a question — (and almost every year it is discussed) — is painful and embarrassing to a man of sensibility. And the possibility that sooner or later these efforts of Demagogues may be successful in actually destroying the independent tenure of the Judicial office — must make him exceedingly loath to place himself in so precarious a position.

In November the North Carolina House elected him to the vacancy by a wide margin over an opponent who waved the menace of his Catholicity in a futile attempt to derail him.

Along with the nullification doctrine, the issue of slavery was highly sensitive to defenders of Southern culture. It was a matter which Gaston had to address very soon after joining the Court, in the landmark 1834 case, *State v. Will*. As a private citizen, Gaston's feelings about the institution were decidedly jaundiced, as he made known in the address to the Chapel Hill students cited above. Hoping that his hearers might soon provide for "the mitigation and, (is it too much to hope for in North Carolina) for the ultimate extirpation of the worst evil that afflicts the Southern part of our Confederacy," he also charged that:

> It is slavery which, more than any other cause, keeps us back in the career of improvement. It stifles industry and suppresses enterprise; it is fatal to economy and prudence; it discourages skill, impairs our strength as a community, and poisons morals at the fountainhead.

In saying that, he was no more than echoing a fairly common Catholic viewpoint, one which was espoused, for example, by Bishop England. And yet Gaston himself owned a number of slaves, though he saw to it that they were baptized and went out of his way to insure that members of slave families were not separated from one another. A testimonial read by representatives of the black community of New Bern on the occasion of Gaston's death gives ample evidence of the esteem in which he was held among them. They speak of him as "our neighbor, our friend and kind protector," and go on to say:

> Judge Gaston was an example in word and conversation, in spirit and purity. He was a friend of the widow and the orphan. He was a kind and indulgent master—the most of his servants can read and write, the consequence is they are a most intelligent set of people. Judge Gaston was a friend of emancipation, he not only emancipated several of his own people, but he bought others and set them free. He was a Christian in deed and truth; his religion was not a thing of form and decencies, it was a pervading principle that entered into all his concerns, all his thoughts and all his hopes.

Within the old Maryland Catholic tradition, in fact, slave ownership was quite common, the difference between the slaves under Catholic (especially clerical) and non-Catholic ownership being largely one of treatment. In 1749 Father George Hunter proclaimed during a retreat:

> Charity to negroes is due from all, particularly their masters. As they are members of Jesus Christ, redeemed by His precious blood, they are to be dealt with in a charitable, christian, paternal manner, which is at the same time a great means to bring them to their duty to God and therefore to gain their souls.

The famous French missionary in Kentucky, Stephen Badin, himself an owner of slaves, in 1805 offered this contrasting view of how non-Catholic masters treated their slaves:

> One could very well ask how the people who follow the principles of Calvin, which predominate here, and who profess to put all men on the same level, can reconcile these without embarrassment, with the traffic in negroes whom they treat almost like animals, whose services they receive every day of the year without giving them either instruction or compensation, whom they feed with coarse food and dress meagerly.

The general Catholic position on slavery in the United States could be summarized by stating that the system was not looked upon as intrinsically immoral, but as a social blight which should be done away with gradually, so that both the Southern whites and blacks would not suffer the dislocating effects of sudden total emancipation. But the problem yet remained for a conscientious Catholic such as Gaston to interpret the law as a Supreme Court Justice in accordance with the dictates of both natural law reasoning and the given statutes of the state.

The case in which he did so was one where a slave named Will had killed an overseer and was sentenced to die by a judge, that verdict being appealed to the State Supreme Court. Evidence brought up in the trial indicated that the overseer had intended to wantonly kill the slave, who responded in self-defense. The trial judge condemned him, referring to an earlier Supreme Court ruling (written before Gaston's entry to the Court), which held that "the power of the master must be absolute to render the submission of the slave perfect." Gaston disagreed, and overturned the ruling. He observed unequivocally:

> It is certain that the master has not the right to slay his slave, and I hold it to be equally certain that the slave has a right to defend himself against the unlawful attempt of his master to deprive him of life.

The branding of the slave's actions in defense of himself as murder also elicited this comment from him:

> I will not presume an arbitrary and inflexible rule so sanguinary in its character and so repugnant to the spirit of those holy statutes which "rejoice the heart, enlighten the eyes, and are true and righteous altogether." If the Legislature should ever prescribe such a law — a supposition which can scarcely be made without disrespect — it will be for those who then sit in the judgment seat to administer it. But the appeal here is to the common law, which declares passion, not transcending all reasonable limits, to be distinct from malice.

The decision had beneficial repercussions in future years, for the very judge who laid down the iron rule of submission in the earlier ruling, followed Gaston's lead in a similar case in 1839, totally reversing his own previous opinion. And Henry Connor, a later Justice of the North Carolina Court who took a scholarly interest in the life of his great predecessor, wrote:

> This great opinion of Judge Gaston's in its clear analysis of the respective legal rights of master and slave, its condemnation of the brutality too often shown towards the

helpless, its sublime compassion for the hunted and terrified
slave, sounded the key-note that never ceased to ring in
North Carolina jurisprudence.

Gaston further expanded the limited rights of blacks by declaring
all free blacks or manumitted slaves to be full citizens of the
state, a right the state's attorney general had refused to
recognize. This opinion was cited by a U.S. Supreme Court
Justice in his dissent from the *Dred Scott* decision.

Similarly, he attempted to elevate the citizenry's view of the
worth of human life, judging an officer who killed a prisoner over
a misdemeanor to be guilty of murder. He admonished a society
which still championed the summary dispatch of wrongdoers:

> There is a recklessness — a wanton disregard of humanity
> and social duty — in taking or endeavoring to take the life
> of a fellow being in order to save oneself from a
> comparatively slight wrong — which is essentially wicked
> and which the law abhorred.

In 1835, North Carolina held a statewide convention to
consider alterations to its state constitution, and Judge Gaston
was elected the representative of Craven County, where New
Bern is located. One injustice he tried to avert was the
convention's abrogation of the right of suffrage for free blacks.
Two amendments that he put forward to preserve their rights as
citizens were narrowly defeated.

After engaging in warm debate over various other
restructurings, Gaston participated in the deliberations on the
revision of the religious test which, though ignored by polite
society, still was technically enshrined as state law. And of course
not all public figures could be accounted members of polite
society. The Presbyterian minister Robert Breckinridge, for
instance, wrote in the Baltimore *Literary and Religious Magazine*
the very month of the convention debate:

> Now, Mr. Gaston, is at this moment, a Judge of the Court of

Appeals of North Carolina. Before he took his seat on the
bench, he took an oath, in some usual form, to support the
constitution of that state. Part of that constitution, asserts
and assumes, the truth of the Protestant religion. But, Mr.
Gaston is an avowed, and most decided Papist! — Now, will
he do himself the justice, mankind the favour and his
religion the service, of explaining this conduct? . . . It cannot
be denied, that this clause in the constitution of North
Carolina, was meant and supposed to exclude, the peculiar
principles of the Roman faith . . .

Judge Gaston himself declined to dignify Rev. Breckinridge
with a response, writing to a correspondent that "the style of the
article was so uncourteous, and the temper which it breathed so
malignant, that self-respect utterly forbade me from paying any
notice to it." Breckinridge, however, continued to air his charges,
suggesting that Gaston had gone to the Archbishop of Baltimore
to obtain a dispensation to perjure himself by violating his oath to
uphold the constitution. Eventually, Gaston's friend, Bishop
England, took up his defense, observing that the legality and
propriety of a Catholic accepting a post had been established by
lawyers and by himself as the ordinary with jurisdiction (not
Baltimore) in three separate cases prior to Gaston's election to
the Judgeship. He finished his vindication of Judge Gaston with
a flourish which the Rev. Breckinridge well merited:

We have heard some persons charge R. J. Breckinridge with having taken his peculiar mode of polemics for
the purpose of attracting more attention, and getting better
supported by his party, whilst others excused him on the
plea of a peculiarity of head. To us, it matters nothing
whither he acts from calculation, from insanity, or from
delusion. We leave him and his vile and vulgar productions,
to their admirers, whilst we deeply regret the connexion,
even as a calumniator, of the name of R. J. Breckinridge,
with that of Will Gaston.

Back at the convention, a number of legislators remarked on
the anachronism of the law, and on its imprecision in specifying

the variety of Protestantism to be held up as the paradigm. One delegate called his colleagues' attention to Gaston's service on the Court as proof that the old prohibition was outmoded:

> A distinguished member of this Convention publicly professing and openly avowing the doctrines of the Catholic Church has been recently appointed by the Assembly to one of the highest judicial stations in the state. Profoundly learned in the law, and eminently skilled in the solution of constitutional questions; of irreproachable character and fastidiously scrupulous in matters of conscience; of retired habits; not seeking but declining office, he accepted the appointment in obedience to the public will.

Gaston himself gave a masterful speech on the need for toleration in which he alluded to his own faith:

> It is not easy for a man to speak of himself or of his principles without disgusting egotism. It will be enough for me to say, that trained from infancy to worship God according to the usages, and carefully instructed in the creed of the most ancient and numerous society of Christians in the world, after arrival at mature age, I deliberately embraced from conviction the faith which had been early instilled into my mind by maternal piety. Without, as I trust, offensive ostentation, I have felt myself bound outwardly to profess what I inwardly believe, and am therefore an avowed though unworthy member of the Roman Catholic Church.

He went on to proclaim before his colleagues the principle of religious toleration and evenhandedness which he espoused, and which he hoped North Carolina would soon espouse:

> I am opposed, out and out, to any interference of the State with the *opinions* of its citizens, and more especially with their opinions on Religious subjects. The good order of society requires that *actions* and *practices* injurious to the public peace and public morality, should be restrained, and but a moderate portion of practical good sense is required to enable the proper authorities to decide what conduct is really thus injurious.

He then defended the Catholic Church from the calumnious charges which lay behind the tenacious defense of Article XXXII. The sacrament of confession, the right of the Church to dispense individuals from vows, the duty owed to the Pope, etc., were topics which militant Protestant propagandists had quarried to portray the Church of Rome as the enemy of the Republic. With an impressive display of learning in apologetics, doctrine and history Gaston rebutted the distortions and sought to open the minds of recalcitrant legislators to a noble principle. "I hope and trust," he finally said in an appeal to their love of *patria*:

> ...that North Carolina will shake off the reproach of lagging behind the other States of the Union, behind the lately enlightened States of Europe, and behind even the spirit of the age, by incorporating into her fundamental institution the principle of perfect Religious freedom. I protest against all partial and mitigated reforms of the doctrine of Intolerance. Of course, I must accept the *most* that can be obtained, but I shall not be content with any thing short of the total abrogation of Religious Tests.

On the other side of the question stood those who still mistrusted Catholics as potential subverters of liberty, one delegate even expressing the opinion that he would rather keep a single honest Catholic out of office in order to keep the one hundred dishonest ones out. An amendment, backed by Gaston, was put forward to strike all religious tests for prospective state office-holders, but it was defeated. Finally a compromise replacing the word "Protestant" with "Christian" gained approval. Gaston was dissatisfied with it, averring that the constitution "ought to have guaranteed the most unlimited freedom of opinion just as long as they did not disturb the peace of a city by their conduct."

By this stage of his career, Gaston, nearing sixty, was being considered for a number of higher national posts. When his old friend John Marshall, who had years earlier heard Gaston argue cases while presiding as a Federal District Court judge in Raleigh, died in 1835, it was rumored that he hoped Gaston would succeed him. The two were close enough friends that it had also been hoped that Gaston would write Marshall's biography. As it turned out, President Jackson nominated Roger Taney, whose political ties with the administration were much closer than the veteran Federalist's. If one puts stock in an anti-Jacksonian paper, Gaston's candidacy was never a serious likelihood. Wrote the New York *Courier*:

> No possible chance for the country under its present misrule to be blessed with such a man upon the Supreme Bench. He is too pure a patriot and too good a man, and possesses too much fitness for the station, to be thought of for a moment at the White House.

He also could have had a seat in the U.S. Senate had he desired it; the legislature would have appointed him without question, for he was the state's most distinguished citizen. Universities poured honorary degrees on him, Harvard, Princeton, Yale and Georgetown among them, and vied to hear him address their graduates. After William Henry Harrison was elected President in 1840, the North Carolina Whigs hoped to gain for him the position of Secretary of State. But when Harrison did offer him the Attorney Generalship, he declined, citing his continued debt of service to North Carolina. Neither the Senate nor the Cabinet could lure him from a station in life "as important to the public welfare as any services which I could render in the political station" being proffered.

In the advance positioning for the nominations in 1844, Gaston's name again surfaced, as an attractive vice presidential candidate running with his one time foe, Henry Clay, now a fellow Whig. But that speculation was given no opportunity to mature, because the judge's health deteriorated somewhat in 1843. Then on January 23, 1844, midway through a normal court day's work, he became ill, sliding into a stroke-induced unconsciousness as he was taken to his office. He then rallied, and engaged in lively conversation with his colleagues who had gathered around him. The discussion turned to free-thinkers and he observed that "A belief in an over-ruling Divinity, who shapes our ends, whose eye is upon us, and who will reward us according to our deeds, is necessary. We must believe there is a God — All wise and ..." Those were his last spoken thoughts, for he then relapsed and died within minutes.

Reactions to his death poured in from around the state and around the country. Gaston was uniformly praised for his integrity, his judicial astuteness, and for the role he played in extending religious and civil liberties. His co-religionists could especially hail him for being a shining example in a state which was none too populated with Catholics. All the exclamations on his virtues are true enough; where the eulogizing tended toward hyperbole was in the confident predictions of his immortality. Arguably Gaston is the greatest statesman North Carolina has ever produced, but Carolinians have given scant notice to his memory. Recent histories of the state relegate him to a single reference or so, and but for the name of a lake near the Virginia border, and a town west of Charlotte whose murder rate would make Gaston blush to be associated with it, the later reminiscence that "his name is a household word in every town and hamlet" rings rather hollow.

But that would matter little to a man who was remarkably devoid of vanity. Surely he would count it better not to be remembered, but to have interpreted the law so that people of all races could be accorded more dignity in the future. And better also than publicity to have aided materially the progress of the Church, while quietly bringing his Protestant colleagues to the realization that Catholics were a far cry from the menace that anti-Papal propaganda had led them to hold in horror.

A devoted Catholic and a true conservative with a strong attachment to a well-ordered society, Gaston was both influential and respected in his day. If his Federalism is antiquated for the twentieth century, his faith and his ethical code are not. He still serves as an exemplar for lawyers and judges who must, as always, assert the permanency of natural law principles even when their professions no longer value them as assiduously as they ought to.

Gaston was invited to compose epitaphs for other distinguished statesmen who preceded him in death. Floridity was in order in those days, so it seems a bit odd that the gravestone above his remains bears only his name. But words he wrote in a letter to his daughter Susan toward the end of his life might well have been carved on that stone:

> To administer justice in the last resort, to expound and apply the laws for the advancement of right and the suppression of wrong, is an ennobling and indeed a holy office, and the exercise of its functions, while it raises my mind above the mists of the earth, above cares and passions, into a pure and serene atmosphere, always seems to impart fresh vigor to my understanding and a better temper to my whole soul.

Bibliography

Connor, Henry G. "William Gaston," in *Great American Lawyers*, ed. William Draper Lewis. The John Winston Co., 1907, pp. 37-84.

Connor, R.D.W. "William Gaston: A Southern Federalist of the Old South and His Yankee Friends," *Proceedings of the American Antiquarian Society*. Vol. XXXII, October 18, 1933, pp. 381-446.

Ellet, Elizabeth. "Margaret Gaston," in *The Women of the American Revolution*. Vol. II. Haskell House, 1969 reprint, pp. 136-144.

England, John. *The Works of the Right Reverend John England*. Vols. V and VI, ed. Most Rev. Sebastian Messmer. Arthur Clark, 1908.

Gaston, William. *Address to the North Carolina Convention of 1835*. Reprinted in *U.S. Catholic Historical Society Historical Records and Studies*, Vol. XVII, June 1926, pp. 189-244.

Guilday, Peter. *The Life and Times of John England*. 2 vols. The America Press, 1927.

McSweeney, Edward. "Judge William Gaston," *U.S. Catholic Historical Society Historical Records and Studies*. Vol. XVII, June 1926, pp. 172-188.

Melville, Annabelle. *John Carroll of Baltimore*. Scribner's, 1955.

North Carolina Reports. Vol. XVIII, Supreme Court Cases, Dec. 1834-June 1836.

Nuesse, Celestine. *The Social Thought of American Catholics, 1634-1829*. CUA Press, 1945.

Purcell, Richard J. "Judge William Gaston: Georgetown University's First Student," *The Georgetown Law Journal*. Vol. 27, No. 7, May 1939, pp. 839-883.

Ray, Mary Augustina. *American Opinion of Roman Catholicism in the Eighteenth Century*. Octagon Books, 1974 reprint.

Ruffin, Thomas. *The Papers of Thomas Ruffin*. Vol. II, ed. J.G. de Roulhac Hamilton. AMS Press, 1973 reprint.

Schauinger, J. Herman. "A Great Southern Catholic," *U.S. Catholic Historical Society*. Vol. 32, No. 2, 1941, pp. 83-93.

Schauinger, J. Herman. "William Gaston and the Supreme Court of North Carolina," *The North Carolina Historical Review*. Vol. XXI, April 1944, pp. 97-117.

Schauinger, J. Herman. *William Gaston: Carolinian*. Bruce, 1944.

6

Roger Brooke Taney:
Courageous and Controversial Lawyer, Statesman, and Chief Justice of the Supreme Court (1777-1864)

STEPHEN M. KRASON

Since this is a study of Roger Brooke Taney (pronounced "Tawney") the *Catholic* statesman, it will not be a discussion solely of a secular public man, but will also discuss and evaluate his life and controversial career in light of his Catholicism. It particularly will inquire into the influence of the Catholic Faith on his life and the extent to which he conducted his career in conformity to the teachings of his Church. Taney's life proceeds progressively, as we might expect of a successful man, from his early college and legal education, through his early legal and political career, to his tenure as Maryland Attorney General and presidential cabinet member, to finally his long career as Chief Justice of the United States Supreme Court. It can thus be easily divided into distinct periods, essentially chronological, for examination, as will be done here. Moreover, in a biographical sketch of a jurist, a consideration of his life is not sufficient; his judicial opinions must also be examined. This will be done here.

Taney is both a curious and appropriate — or, if one has a different perspective, inappropriate — figure to include in a book about American Catholic statesmen. The word "curious" is used because today few Americans — for that matter, few *Catholic* Americans — are familiar with his life or even his name. Of those who *have* heard of him, most probably do not know that he was Catholic. When people think of Catholic American statesmen, the names of Charles Carroll of Carrollton, Al Smith, and John F. Kennedy readily come to mind, but few think of Roger Brooke Taney.

The reason the inclusion of Taney in a book about American Catholic statesmen is appropriate, or perhaps inappropriate, is because the Supreme Court opinion he authored in *Dred Scott v. Sandford* (1857) resulted in charges that he was not truly a Christian. Those with some knowledge of the history of the period might say that writing a judicial opinion which seems to have endorsed slavery makes it inappropriate to regard Taney as a "Catholic" or "Christian" statesman and include him in this book. Others who may not be familiar with Taney might say, upon hearing of his Catholicism and his role in the *Dred Scott* decision, that he makes a very appropriate subject for inquiry in this book for this *very* fact. That is, they might believe it worth examining how a supposedly Catholic Christian judge could render a decision which seems to be so patently *un*Christian.

We can understand from this why Walker Lewis, whose *Without Fear or Favor* is one of the chief biographies of Taney and a major reference for this essay, refers to his life as an "enigma" and a "tragedy." Let us examine why this was so and exactly what kind of Catholic statesman he actually was.

Early Life and Education

It is ironic that Taney should be remembered as the judge who upheld American slavery when his ancestors who first come to our shores were indentured servants. The first Taneys arrived in Calvert County, Maryland from England around 1660. His mother's side of the family, the Brookes, came from England around 1650. They had been Protestants, but after becoming part of the landed gentry of southern Maryland converted to the faith that was predominant among them, Catholicism. Roger Brooke Taney was born as the Revolutionary War raged — although not touching Calvert county — on March 17, 1777. We do not know a great deal about the influence of Taney's parents on him: we can only make tentative conclusions on the basis of limited facts. He seems to have inherited aspects of each of their temperaments: a tendency to quietness, charitableness, and kindness from his mother and a strong temper from his father. It was also perhaps from her example that he became a lover of nature and beauty and gained the powers of self-control to enable him to so arrest that temper that in later life he came to be viewed as one of the mildest of men. We know that his parents are responsible for his Catholicism because they brought him up in the Faith. We do not know for sure, but we can reasonably surmise that his mother's example may have played a substantial part in his later active spirituality. He wrote about her that "she had knowledge and qualities far higher and better than mere human learning can give." We wonder from those words if he did not perceive that her faith was the source of this.

Except for his temper, Taney appears to have had little in common with his father. Unlike his son, Michael Taney never appears to have won the struggle for self-control. He is described by Lewis as "a hard-riding, hard-drinking, hail-fellow-well-met" and his temper resulted, late in his life, in his stabbing a neighbor to death and having to flee the State of Maryland. Nevertheless, if Taney owes his temperament primarily to his mother, he owes his ultimate journey into public life to his father. Not only did Michael Taney see to it that Roger got a good education, but his firm belief in primogeniture insured that his younger sons — Roger was the second of four sons — prepared for the professions. By choosing law for Roger and later steering him into politics, Michael Taney unknowingly set him on the path to the highest judicial office in the country.

Most of Roger Taney's schooling before college was by private tutors hired by his father. The manner of education his father chose for him seems curious. The Taneys, like all Catholics in Maryland before the American Revolution, were subjected to religious persecution at the hands of the predominant Puritans. If religious persecution has usually caused Catholics to become insular and defensive, however, it did not so affect Michael Taney. Most of the teachers he selected for his son seem to have been non-Catholics, the most important having been trained under Presbyterian auspices at Princeton (Presbyterianism is related to the creed of the Puritans, the very group which persecuted Maryland's Catholics). He later chose a Presbyterian college, Dickinson, for his son. The lack of Catholic schools, or for that matter, any schools nearby may have been the reason for Michael Taney's particular decisions about the pre-college education of his son. His choice of Dickinson appears to have resulted from his hearing of its good reputation and his dissatisfaction with the quality of the Catholic higher education he had received in Europe.

We do not know if Taney practiced his Catholic Faith when at Dickinson. It does not appear, however, that his Presbyterian higher education caused him to move away from Catholicism. What we do know is that Taney was a very good student at Dickinson, was well regarded by his teachers, and that his residence there profoundly influenced his life. He got a solid education under such teachers as Dr. Charles Nisbet, a Presbyterian minister and the first president of Dickinson who gained much renown because of the accomplishment of so many of the graduates of that small college, and Charles Huston, who later became a member of the Pennsylvania Supreme Court and may have further inspired Taney toward a legal career. An additional source of influence on Taney was the outbreak of the Whiskey Rebellion, which swirled around Carlisle, Pennsylvania, where Dickinson was located. Dr. Nisbet gained the wrath of the local citizens by his strident defense of President Washington's administration during the rebellion and seems to have influenced the students. Also, President Washington stayed in the town for a week while leading the militia westward to break up the rebellion. This display of power on the part of the new national government for the purpose of upholding one of its laws (albeit an unpopular one), coupled with Dr. Nisbet's open insistence on the necessity of public order and good government, may have influenced Taney both in the short-term, by moving him toward the Federalist party, and in the long-run in shaping his commitment to the importance of public order and the rule of law in making republican government work.

Taney was graduated from Dickinson in 1795 and shortly thereafter began his legal education. The practice in those days was for a student to read law in the office of a lawyer or judge for three years, acting as a sort of apprentice. Then, if qualified, he would be recommended for admission to the state's bar by the man he studied under. Taney studied law under Judge Jeremiah Townley Chase in Annapolis. Annapolis was the state capital and the center of the activity of the Maryland Bar. It was there that Taney observed such outstanding early American lawyers as Luther Martin and William Pinkney in action. Both became Attorneys General of Maryland and Pinkney also became United States Attorney General. These men became professional models for him and stirred his ambitions, which were always much more directed toward reaching the peak of the legal profession than toward political life. Late in his life, Taney was to write that his highest ambition had been to become Attorney General of Maryland, a position then viewed as the highest honor a lawyer in his state could receive.

At Annapolis, Taney was a diligent student, reading law twelve hours a day and turning down social invitations. One wonders if his quietness and discomfort in large groups did not motivate his reluctance to mingle in Annapolis society as much as his concern about his legal education. One of his biographers suggests yet another reason: Taney wanted to avoid his father who was likely to turn up at Annapolis social functions — and to arrange to have his son invited also — because he was a very sociable member of the House of Delegates (the lower house of the Maryland legislature). This would indicate that Taney was not close to his father, which would not be surprising in light of the difference in their temperaments discussed above. This lack of closeness might also be suggested by the fact that he speaks so fondly of his mother in his unfinished "Memoir," but, except for facts, says nothing about his father. Every indication is that Taney was a dutiful and obedient son and there is no evidence that he lacked love or affection for his father. It is likely that whatever distance existed between them was due to Taney's recognition of their temperamental differences and his desire, in spite of his always seeming to accede to his father's education and career wishes for him, to establish himself on his own.

Even with his general unwillingness to socialize, Taney made friends in Annapolis. One of them was Francis Scott Key, also studying law there, who found his own niche in American history. It was through him that Taney met Key's sister Anne, who later became his wife.

Early Legal and Political Career

Taney was admitted to the Maryland bar on June 19, 1799. Two days later, he tried his first case. It was in the Mayor's Court in Annapolis, a court presided over by the mayor of the town who in this case was unlearned in the law. It is worth noting this debut because he was so nervous he had to fold his arms over his chest and lean against the table in front of him to control his trembling. This was a serious problem for Taney early in his legal career and, he indicates in his "Memoir," was not completely overcome even later on. He wrote that this tendency to extreme nervousness was of such a concern to him in his early career that he was not sure he should stay in law, although he "never for a moment thought of engaging in any other pursuit." This anxiety when speaking publicly was probably due to the same discomfort with social situations as was seen in his reluctance to attend social functions in his law student days. It was also foreshadowed in the considerable difficulty he had standing before a crowd to deliver the valedictory address at his Dickinson commencement. It seems curiously odd when one considers how strong and forceful he would be later in his career in the controversies he faced in Andrew Jackson's cabinet and on the Supreme Court.

We detect in Taney's character a tendency to lack confidence. This is seen not only in his timidity in public and social situations, but also in his occasional references throughout his life to his frail bodily constitution. We can only speculate as to the reason for this. Perhaps it was due to his generally quiet nature or his feeling slightly inadequate when seeing his personality alongside his father's or because of the tender treatment given him by the women — first his mother and sisters and later his wife and six daughters — who surrounded him in his life. Whichever, it is likely that Taney's lack of confidence was not a serious handicap in light of his later accomplishments. We may even be tempted to overestimate it because of the great humility which he showed in his dealings with people and in his writings about himself in his "Memoir" and correspondence.

Another noteworthy thing about Taney's first case is the fact that he gave some thought to whether he should defend a man who might be guilty. This is hardly a concern to most present-day lawyers, who have been schooled in a post-Holmesian environment which believes that law is separated from morality. It is a small indication, however, that he brought a moral sense into his profession with him that was probably due to his religious upbringing. He decided that defending the man in this case was justifiable, even though he referred to him in a letter as "as great a scoundrel as ever lived," because "what he had done was only a private fraud, and not a felony in the eye of the law" and "every man ought to be punished only according to the laws of his country." His client was acquitted.

Very shortly after this case, he returned to the family plantation, even though he had said that Calvert County was not a good place to start a law practice of its predominantly rural character. He went back there apparently to please his father, who had plans to run him for the House of Delegates. He might also have been motivated to return by a lack of certainty about where in Maryland to begin a practice. Even if Taney were reluctant about running, which is not certain, he should have been very pleased that his father selected him instead of his older brother — who only later got into the Legislature — for this.

The campaign, if one could call it that, consisted primarily of how successful a candidate could be at soliciting votes when the voters came to the polls on the four days of the balloting. It might not be surprising, in light of what has already been said, that Taney viewed these as an anxious four days, especially since the voting was *viva voce* and a candidate always knew how the tally stood. In spite of his social shortcomings and the fact that, as he wrote in his "Memoir," he "knew very few of the voters even by name," he was one of those elected. He wrote that he had been "gratified, greatly gratified at the result: yet I was not overelated"; because he won, he believed, not so much because of his own efforts as those of a few energetic and determined friends. We see a sign here of the humility spoken of above.

Taney appears to have taken an active role in the session of the Legislature to which he was elected. Although a freshman, he was named to a number of committees — there were special committees, not standing committees, in legislatures then — and was even made chairman of some. His legal training probably was responsible for this, since in those days state legislatures were not dominated by lawyers. He wrote that at the session he "was listened to with respect and attention."

Lewis suggests that the political life began to appeal to

Taney and he started to dream of his future in politics. The election of 1800 caused his bubble to burst, however. The bitter Jefferson-Adams contest for the Presidency resulted in a successful move by the Democratic-Republicans in Jefferson's home state of Virginia to change state law to benefit their candidate by having all the state's presidential electors selected on a state-wide basis. When the Federalists in Maryland tried the same thing to benefit Adams, they aroused intense public opposition. Taney, as a Federalist, was caught in the middle of this and lost in his attempt to be reelected to the House of Delegates.

This defeat motivated Taney to seriously set himself down to establishing a law practice. He tells us that he consulted his father closely about this and Michael Taney must have been understanding about the limitations of Calvert County. He suggested Baltimore. Taney, however, believed that Frederick was a more promising place for a young lawyer at the time and chose to go there. We see in this that Taney, irrespective of the differences between their personalities, really respected and trusted his father and his father must have understood his needs. We also can observe an assertion of the young man's independence.

Some might be tempted to think that a motivating factor in Taney's choosing Frederick was the presence there of Anne Key, his future wife. We have no evidence of this, however, and it was five years before they were married.

Taney practiced law in Frederick for twenty-two years, gradually becoming a leader of the bar there. Lewis says that Taney succeeded not because of extraordinary gifts of eloquence, charisma, wit, or charm — which some men have been able to rely on — but because he had "a mind of exceptional clarity, a scholarly love of the law and a life-long devotion to truth and justice." His strong determination compensated for a physical frailty that sometimes caused him to become ill after a particularly demanding case.

No effort will be made to survey the major cases Taney handled in his legal career at Frederick. Only a few will be singled out which have a noteworthy ethical dimension and can thereby shed light on Taney as a Catholic statesman and Catholic lawyer. It was mentioned before that Taney seemed concerned in his first case about whether he should defend a man he thought guilty. It was, as mentioned, to Taney's credit that he considered this and the fact he felt almost apologetic about going ahead to defend the man afterwards indicates Taney's strong moral sensitivity. When he got settled into his practice in Frederick, he apparently put aside this sensitivity and decided that it was his responsibility to defend a client regardless of whether he thought him guilty. He developed the conviction that it was a lawyer's job to defend his client as best as he knew how and to leave it up to the judge and jury to decide guilt or innocence.

Three important cases of Taney's during the time of his practice in Frederick illustrate this. These were all criminal cases, even though most of his practice involved civil cases. One was the case of Thomas Burk, a black man charged with the rape of a ten-year-old white girl. Taney brought Luther Martin into the case to assist him, and the two poured themselves intensely into it, even to the point of Martin's stimulating the anger of the judge. They lost, and Burk was sentenced to hang. Their appeals failed, but Burk escaped from jail before the sentence could be carried out.

The second case was that of General James Wilkinson. This case is complicated, so it will be explained only briefly here. Wilkinson was court-martialed on the charge that while commanding general of the U.S. Army he had been in the pay of Spain. He was closely aligned with Jefferson, had many enemies, and was an opportunist and manipulator. Among other escapades, he was a cohort of Aaron Burr's in the latter's ill-fated attempt to establish a southwestern empire which led to his trial for treason. He abandoned Burr when he saw greater advantage for himself in revealing the plot to Jefferson, and became Burr's chief accuser at his trial. Wilkinson may have been guilty of the charges brought against him in the court-martial, but he convinced Taney and his co-counsel of his innocence. Having kept his documentation and planned his case for years in anticipation of a court-martial, he carried out much of his own defense at the proceeding and was found "Not Guilty." Taney and his colleague decided not to charge Wilkinson a fee because of what they believed to be their initial misjudgment of him.

The final case was that of the Reverend Jacob Gruber, a Methodist minister from Pennsylvania, who was indicted for instigating slaves "to commit acts of mutiny and rebellion" in a sermon he delivered in Washington County, Maryland, in 1818. This was the type of law that invites varied interpretations as to its meaning and is difficult to prove has been violated. Perhaps Reverend Gruber's sermon, fiery and severe as it was, did constitute instigation of slaves, especially since they were among the persons in the audience. A major issue was precisely what the Reverend said in the sermon, and testimony about this conflicted. He was acquitted.

The other point to note about each of these cases was that Taney was not reluctant, even at a point in his career when he was a prominent and well established member of the bar, to take the cases of unpopular defendants. A lawyer risks his own popularity in doing this, and Taney's willingness shows both an admirable courage and a commitment to the proper view of the lawyer's responsibilities, as he understood it. In considering this, however, one must realize that there is nothing virtuous, from a Christian perspective, about courage in the defense of unpopular causes, but only in defense of rightful causes. While one can understand the necessity of at least some lawyers' willingness to defend guilty clients and those involved in unpopular causes which are not necessarily for rightful things, he must also wonder if a Christian lawyer can go ahead and do these things if Christian morality is harmed in the process. We may thus be motivated to think that Taney should have allowed his early reluctance to continue.

Legal Career in Baltimore
and Attorney Generalship of Maryland

With the incapacity of Luther Martin and the death of William Pinkney, Roger Taney was able to assume a place of leadership in the Maryland bar. In 1823, Taney moved his family to Baltimore to be at the heart of the Maryland legal and commercial scene. It was during this time that Taney began to appear as a advocate before the U.S. Supreme Court. One of the cases he brought to the high court, according to one of his biographers, probably helped shape his later political and judicial career. This was *Etting v. Bank of the United States*, decided in 1826. James W. McCulloh, cashier of the Bank's Baltimore branch, the Bank's president, and one of its directors speculated heavily in its stock. They helped themselves to the Bank's funds and covered up the accounts. They got to the point of owing the Bank 3.5 million dollars. The Bank's Board of Directors demanded security and McCulloh persuaded some Baltimore businessmen, including Solomon Etting, to endorse notes for him in the amount of $12,500 each. While McCulloh was lining up this business support, the directors suppressed the fact that he had misused funds and falsified Bank records. They let him hold his post until these notes were delivered, then fired him. When the facts about the whole affair finally became known, the businessmen refused to pay and the Bank sued one of them, Etting, to have him pay the money owed on the note he signed. (Etting was singled out because of an agreement that the decision would bind the other businessmen as well.) Taney was retained as counselor for Etting and argued that he had been deliberately misled by the Bank, whose directors knew that McCulloh could get persons to endorse the notes only if he remained as cashier and only if he made what amounted to false representations as to his need for financial assistance. Taney said that they undoubtedly planned to dismiss him all along, but first wanted to be sure he had secured the endorsers. The Bank responded that it did not have an obligation to protect Etting and he should have taken greater care.

The trial court agreed with the Bank, and Taney, with Daniel Webster's help, took the case to the U.S. Supreme Court. The Supreme Court divided 3 to 3, thereby sustaining the trial court judgment. The case went to a second trial, but finally the Bank settled out of court with the businessmen.

It is likely that Taney's experience with the Bank of the United States in the case — wherein he saw its willingness to be unfairly self-interested, deceptive, and manipulative — along with his involvement with state banks in Maryland which disliked the Bank of the United States, shaped his later ardent opposition to it as a member of Jackson's cabinet and led to the active role he played in Jackson's veto of the Bank's rechartering (which will be discussed shortly).

Another case that Taney took in his private practice in Baltimore was the Barnum divorce case. I shall not go into the facts of the case, except to say that it involved one Sarah Gilmor Barnum who was a friend of Taney's and who both came from and married into Baltimore merchant wealth. Sarah's elopement at age sixteen with David Strong Barnum began a period of difficult relations with his family, which included their attempts to control the couple's life and their spreading of nasty rumors about her seeing other men. Her husband sought a divorce from her, which in those days had to be gotten from the legislature, not the courts. The ensuing proceedings in the legislature were something of a *cause celebre*, with Taney being convinced that Sarah's reputation was being unjustly blackened in the process. Taney used some of the influence he had in the legislature to get the testimony against her before the Committee on Divorces suppressed and in getting it to award *her* a partial divorce (from bed and board).

The reason I believe this case is important to speak about here is because of its specific subject matter. The Catholic Church, of which Taney was a member, teaches that divorce is immoral. It is true that Sarah Gilmor Barnum was not Catholic, so for her the moral question may not have seemed pertinent (this is irrespective, of course, of the natural law's prohibition of divorce which applies to everyone). A serious question must be raised, however, about whether it was right for Taney, a Catholic, to assist another person to get a divorce. Problem enough can be raised about a lawyer doing this in a dispassionate way for a person who was merely a client, but Taney additionally viewed himself as helping a friend and his behavior during the proceedings showed that it clearly was not just a dispassionate undertaking for him. While it is true that he was just helping her to get a *legal* divorce, as opposed to seeking to have her church dissolve the bond, the moral question still is pertinent because the same potential for emotional and familial damage exists in either case and the availability of legal divorce tends to weaken the aura of sanctity of marriage and the family unit which religion has long sought to protect. Nevertheless, the fact that Taney only helped her to get a "partial" divorce from bed and board indicates that he did not do anything wrong since the Catholic Church is sometimes willing to accept this kind of legal action so long as the parties — assuming they had a church wedding in the first place — do not remarry.

One important case that Taney handled for the state as attorney general was *Brown v. Maryland* in 1827. This case raised the question of whether the commerce clause of the U.S. Constitution prohibited an annual license fee imposed by the State of Maryland on importers of certain wholesale goods. The Supreme Court, with Chief Justice Marshall writing the opinion, held that it did so prohibit. Marshall enunciated the "original package" doctrine, stating that the Constitution did not permit a tax upon any goods while they remained the property of the importer in their original package. Taney's own view of the tax was not pertinent, since his duty as attorney general required that he defend the state's position. Nevertheless, he indicated that he agreed with it, and this perhaps reflected a turning point away from his previous Federalist views and a gradual movement toward the principles of Jacksonian democracy. It also presaged his later unwillingness as Chief Justice to take the broad view of the commerce clause — which was the subject of a substantial amount of constitutional adjudication under John Marshall and Taney — that Marshall did. (He did come to agree with Marshall, however, about the "original package" doctrine).

Member of President Andrew Jackson's Cabinet — The Controversy over the Rechartering of the Bank of the United States

Taney was called upon by Andrew Jackson to serve his Cabinet as United States Attorney General in 1831. This was in the third year of Jackson's administration and came about after a conflict with John C. Calhoun's (his Vice-President) supporters in his cabinet — resulting from, of all things, tensions on the Washington social scene — led him to ask for the resignations of virtually his entire original Cabinet. Taney later wrote that he accepted the appointment with reluctance because of his admiration for Jackson and sympathy with him because of the difficulties caused him both by his enemies and supposed friends. He took over an office whose responsibilities were demanding, but whose staff consisted merely of one clerk and one messenger.

It was not long before Taney found himself embroiled in the controversy surrounding the rechartering of the second Bank of the United States. This matter is by far the one that Taney's Cabinet career is most remembered for and was the thing first responsible for making him a sizable number of political enemies. As a prelude to the discussion of this, a few words about the bank's stormy history are in order.

Almost from its beginning, the Bank attracted a bevy of speculators out to enrich themselves, even if it be at the public's expense. Fiscally conservative and public-spirited merchants such as Stephen Girard of Philadelphia had purchased most of the Bank's stock, but because of a loophole in its charter they — like all the stockholders — could have no more than thirty votes. Speculators who individually owned a relatively small number of shares got control of the bank by doing things like a group of them from Baltimore did: placing 40,141 shares in the names of 15,628 individuals, with a power of attorney from each. They then had many times more votes than Girard with his large investment had. When these speculators got the power, they manipulated the Bank's operations and policies to enrich themselves on its payroll, making themselves liberal loans and speculating further in its stock. This led to scandals like the one in the *Etting* case. These problems were coupled with the Bank's history of weak and incompetent leadership.

The Bank was "cleaned up" after the very able Nicholas Biddle of Philadelphia took its helm. Biddle was one of the top bankers in the country, but was also autocratic. He effectively appointed most of the Bank's board of directors, controlled its committees, and used his extreme personableness to great advantage. His views about the economy and monetary policy — especially his emphasis on paper money — and the Bank's dominance over state banks and its influence in Congress, put him on a collision course with Jackson. One also cannot underestimate the role that the large egos of two strong-willed men had in shaping the conflict.

According to Lewis, Taney saw the issue squarely as one involving the protection of basic principles of democratic government. Lewis says that for Taney "the power of the Bank constituted a threat to the rights and independence of free citizens, and indeed to the government itself." Taney seemed to view it as some kind of monster stretching its tentacles ever farther over the landscape of the nation.

The bank's charter did not expire until 1836, but thinking it had a substantial amount of support in Congress its board decided to seek rechartering before the end of Jackson's first term in 1833. Most of the members of Jackson's second Cabinet, Taney excepted, supported the Bank. Biddle even used his influence with Jackson's Secretary of the Treasury, Louis McLane, to have him recommend the bank's rechartering to Congress in his annual report. If Biddle and other allies of the Bank favored the early push for rechartering because they thought the Bank would win, Taney favored it because he thought it would lose. If Jackson vetoed Congressional rechartering of the Bank, Taney reasoned, the issue would then be in the forefront of the 1832 campaign and Jackson's reelection would be a verdict against the Bank. If the rechartering did not come up at that point, the Bank could quietly use its not inconsiderable influence to try to defeat Jackson and then to also quietly get the rechartering passed afterwards when there would be no serious debate about it.

As the rechartering bill was moving through Congress in the summer of 1832, it was uncertain what Jackson would do. Taney did not wait for him to consult his Cabinet before setting out his recommendations in writing to him. Taney later said that he wrote the President that "the Bank was unconstitutional and inexpedient, and that it had abused its powers, was dangerous to the liberties of the country, and that the menacing and offensive manner in which the renewal was demanded made it the more necessary that the President should meet it by a direct and decisive veto."

When the bill came to Jackson, Taney was in Annapolis on business. Jackson wrote him to return to Washington as soon as he could; he wanted Taney's help in preparing his veto message. He needed Taney's assistance because his other Cabinet members had declined to give it unless he used language in the veto message that they found acceptable. The final draft of the message appears to have been a collaborative endeavor of Amos Kendall, a long-time Jackson supporter who had a post in the Treasury Department, Andrew Donelson, Jackson's close aide and nephew through marriage, Levi Woodbury, the Secretary of the Navy who was later to serve on the Supreme Court with Taney, and Taney. An important contribution of Taney's was the contention that the Bank was unconstitutional because it was not a "necessary and proper" means of implementing powers of the national government which were specifically enumerated in the Constitution.

There was a second part to the Bank crisis after the recharter veto in which Taney figured even more prominently and which was even more responsible for bringing the wrath of Jackson's opponents on him. This was the controversy over whether to withdraw the government's deposits from the Bank. The Bank's charter required that the government's funds be kept in it unless the Secretary of the Treasury directed otherwise. This was of the nature of a contract between the government and the Bank which was unalterable during the life of the charter. The President could not order the Secretary to withdraw the deposits, but only request it. Jackson, having easily secured reelection, decided he wanted the deposits removed, but Secretary McLane was of no mind to do this. This necessitated a Cabinet reshuffle. This took place in May 1833, when McLane was moved up to Secretary of State and, as was part of the condition of his doing so, his friend William J. Duane of Philadelphia was appointed Secretary of the Treasury. Duane did not make it clear if he would comply with a Jackson request to remove the deposits. He hesitated until in late September 1833 he was removed by Jackson and Taney appointed in his place.

On September 25, 1833, Taney issued the order to remove government funds from the Bank. Actually, the order merely began a series of withdrawals to be extended over a considerable period of time. This would minimize the disruption and was also a strategic move aimed at depriving Biddle of any justification for a tight credit policy.

Biddle, however, had already set his plan of action into motion. More than a month before Taney's action he had ordered the Bank to take steps to reduce outstanding loans, drain specie from circulation, and withdraw capital from offices in the West. Biddle made it very clear in his correspondence that he did this for political reasons; he wanted to cause financial hardship in the country in order to pressure Congress to recharter the bank. The last step especially was intended to make Jackson uncomfortable since his political base was in the West. The result of the Bank's actions was to cause an economic panic that triggered a string of bank failures, business collapses, a surge of unemployment, and a slashing of prices and wages. Taney responded with a plan to help state banks stay solvent by transferring government funds in specie to them. All the while the Bank of the United States was getting stronger. The crisis ended only when powerful Eastern political leaders began to attack the Bank and a number of businessmen and bankers in New York City formed a committee to look into causes of the contraction and threatened to expose the Bank for prolonging the panic for political reasons while increasing its own financial strength. At this, Biddle relented and announced that there would be no further contraction. Lewis says that, with that, the Bank lost its battle with Jackson "for by admitting it could control the panic the Bank forfeited its standing."

During the financial crisis engineered by the Bank, Taney was ferociously attacked in Congress and in the press. The three major figures in the Senate, John C. Calhoun, Jackson's first Vice-President, Henry Clay, his 1832 defeated opponent, and Daniel Webster were firmly opposed to Jackson's and Taney's action, but their own inability to agree with each other and Biddle's unwillingness to compromise put the nails in the Bank's coffin. Even if they failed to save the Bank, they got back at Taney — twice. Taney's appointment as Secretary of the

Treasury was an interim one to expire at the end of the 1833 session of Congress unless the Senate confirmed him. It rejected him. This was the first Cabinet appointment ever rejected by the Senate. Later, in 1835, with the memory of the Bank controversy still fresh, the Senate, with Webster acting as the point man, indirectly rejected Jackson's appointment of Taney to an Associate Justiceship on the Supreme Court by voting that it be "indefinitely postponed" at the end of the session. Taney was thus out of the government and stymied in his efforts to continue his public career. He was also the victim of forceful personal attacks in the press, which, among other things, slammed his supposed lack of intelligence, lack of independence from Jackson, and opportunism. He suffered for his loyalty to Jackson and his democratic principles. He was down — but, as we shall see, not out.

A Glimpse at Taney's Personal and Family Life

Before launching into an examination of Taney's career on the Supreme Court and his role in the *Dred Scott* case, it is worth looking more closely at the man personally and at his relations with his family. By doing this we can gain a better insight into what kind of an individual he truly was and how seriously he took his Catholicism and allowed it to shape his everyday life. Contrary to what some Catholic politicians today like to believe, a public official who is Catholic cannot be "Catholic" only in one realm of his life, whether it be the official or the private, and dispense with his Catholicism as the reference point in shaping his actions in the other. We are essentially "whole" men; we cannot subdivide our lives into parts with a different orientation for each part. It is with this understanding that we examine the personal side of Taney here.

Space permits only a brief consideration and no attempt will be made to look at his personal life chronologically. Some noteworthy facts will simply be added to those already mentioned and will be commented on.

Let us first consider his family life. Taney's biographers and the record of his life give every indication of his having had a very good marriage and of his being a loving and devoted husband and father. We can expect nothing more of a Catholic man in this regard. Taney appears to have been genuinely satisfied in his family life and probably received much attention from his wife and six daughters (the Taneys' only son died at age three). Besides his devotion to his wife and children, he gave much help to his extended family. He helped his brother Octavius after his wife died and he became seriously ill. He also assisted his brother Augustus' widow and her children. He also supported his mother and his sisters Dorothy and Sophia, who had to leave Calvert County during the War of 1812.

Taney's Catholicism makes it seem curious that he should marry Anne Key, a devout Episcopalian. It is even more curious that all their daughters were brought up in her faith. The marriage, although a mixed one at a time when that was strongly disapproved by the Church, seems to have had the Church's blessing since he continued to regularly practice his faith and receive the sacraments for the rest of his life. He also appears to have remained in the good graces of the Church's hierarchy as seen by the fact that they called upon him at different times for legal advice.

It has been alleged that there was an agreement between Taney and his wife that all the sons of the marriage would be brought up in Taney's faith and all the daughters in Anne's. Taney's great-grandson, Roger Brooke Taney Anderson, a Protestant minister, confirmed this. Taney biographer Carl Brent Swisher informs us of an article in a Catholic publication early in this century, however, which states that Taney replied to a relative who had asked him about this that he could not have done this as a Catholic. Further, Swisher tells us that the marriage was performed by a Catholic priest and the birth and baptism of the Taney's first child — a daughter — were apparently recorded in the Catholic Church in Taney Town. All in all, it must be concluded that the evidence of such a pre-nuptial agreement is ambiguous.

Agreement or no, we must nevertheless wonder about how the Church, especially in that time, would have accepted the marriage if the children were not being reared Catholic and how committed Taney, who permitted this, was to the teaching and discipline of his Church. We might reasonably speculate that he was advised by his priest that all this was acceptable although Lewis tells us that "[h]e . . . once reproved a priest who sought to press his faith upon the family." Taney may only have done this, however, because the Taneys' marriage was apparently free of religious tension and he wanted to keep it that way. The charity and toleration they had for each other's religions is seen in Anne's always encouraging one of their daughters to go to Church with him so he would not have to go alone and in Taney's participating in the Protestant weddings of his five daughters who lived to adulthood.

In short, questions can certainly be raised about whether Taney was properly assuming his obligations in not raising his children as Catholics. In the absence of established fact, however, we must give him the benefit of the doubt that in his marriage he did what he was probably led to believe was permitted by his Church. It seems likely that if he was willing to follow a Church rule that he be buried in a Catholic cemetery upon his death — he left instructions that he be laid next to his mother — apart from his beloved wife of forty-nine years, that he would have followed the obligations set down by the Church on the more significant matter of marriage.

It has already been stated that Taney had many admirable personal qualities. His ability to control a fiery temper and his charitableness are especially noteworthy. Small incidents in his life give a witness to his charity. One occurred when he was still practicing law in Frederick. Taney, by then an experienced attorney, was the counsel for one side in a property dispute; a young attorney named Ross was the opposing counsel. When the case was called for trial, Ross told the court that he was ready. Taney quietly told him in the courtroom that the land was not accurately described in his court papers and so, because of the legal practice of the time, his case would fail without anything further being considered. This demonstrated Taney's desire to win cases "fair and square" — on the merits — and not on technicalities. Ross never forgot Taney's kindness and one of Taney's biographers tells how years later Ross put down another attorney whose approach to the law was quite the opposite by telling him how the then-Chief Justice refused to take advantage of technicalities.

Also, Taney's charity did not extend only to those on the same social level as him — or of the same race. Those who were later to scorn him for his "unChristian" attitude toward blacks expressed in the *Dred Scott* case would have done well to consider the time he stopped to help a little black girl draw water from a well and then gave her a message to take back reproving the person who sent her because the work was too arduous for her. They might also take note of his practice of humbly waiting in line with poor people, including many blacks, at the confessional, even though his priest had told him he could come in by a special door and also the fact that he voluntarily supported two aged ex-slaves of his family for many years when they had no place to turn.

Little kindnesses, often to perfect strangers, abounded in Taney's life. In his last year, his old parish priest in Frederick told him of a man who cleaned up the area around his mother's grave which had been neglected with the aged Taney living so far away. Taney wrote him and thanked him profusely and signed the letter "your grateful friend."

Another dimension of Taney's humility, as Lewis tells us, was Taney's willingness to admit error. Lewis also suggests that there may have been a limit to his humility, for he could be a stubborn man, especially when he formed a firm judgment. This, Lewis points out, was seen in his relationship with his friend Thomas Ellicott, president of the Union Bank of Maryland. This is a complicated matter and will not be gone into detail here. All that needs to be said is that when decisions had to be made about alternative banks to put the government's deposits into after their withdrawal from the Bank of the United States, Taney and Jackson were repeatedly approached by Ellicott to make the Baltimore-based Union Bank one of the selections. Taney did not select the depository for Baltimore since he was a stockholder in the Union Bank and wished to avoid the appearance of a conflict of interest. He did arrange a meeting between Jackson and Ellicott, and Jackson personally selected the Union Bank. This happened after Ellicott made intense appeals to both and after both were warned against trusting him. These warnings angered Taney, who asserted that he had the fullest confidence in Ellicott. The truth was that Ellicott had been heavily involved in speculation which seriously weakened the Union Bank and also secretly had been propping up an official in the Bank of Maryland. Ellicott's insistence about getting the government deposits was due to his need for them for both of these purposes. Taney believed the best of Ellicott until some occurrences aroused his suspicions. He succeeded in getting an audit of the Union Bank which revealed what was happening. In the meantime, the Bank of Maryland collapsed and set off a chain of other bank failures which aroused indignation at Taney. It was a painful realization for Taney. His stubborn loyalty to Ellicott and unwillingness to listen to what others were trying to say about his long-time friend cost him. Besides stubbornness, some might say that Taney's actions cast doubt on his integrity because he seems to have been nepotistic and used his public position to help his friend Ellicott in at least a limited way. Taney did not, however, act at any point in a manner he believed was contrary to the public good and as soon as he suspected that all might not be right he changed his course.

The episode should not be viewed as one which raises questions about how ethical he was, but simply one which, according to Lewis, "seems to show a blind spot in his judgment."

Actually, unethical conduct was very much the opposite of what was normally associated with Taney. As J. Herman Schauinger writes in his historical sketch of Catholics in American public life, "one of the basic reasons for his [Taney's] success was that all trusted him, that his integrity was known to lawyer, juror, and judge alike."

One other point in this section about Taney's personal life should be considered: the role that he himself saw his Catholicism playing in his life. The indications are that Taney's faith was a source of much strength for him, although perhaps in a quiet way. Joseph Taggart, in an early-twentieth century biographical sketch of Taney, puts it this way:

> The deep religious feeling of the Chief Justice, while it may have been unobserved by those who had occasion to associate with him in the course of business, nevertheless formed the basis of the ruling principle of his life.

Samuel Tyler, who completed Taney's unfinished "Memoir" at his request, wrote the following in it:

> Chief-Justice Taney's religion was the moving principle of his life. It filled him with every Christian grace. Faith, hope, and charity led him in . . . [his] high career.

and:

> In the mysterious drama of human life, there has never yet trod the stage a more chivalric man than Roger B. Taney. The fiery temper of his soul had been chastened by that form of Christianity which is ministered by the Church that sits on the seven hills of Rome, the imperial mistress of the moral order of the modern world. In his Christian faith was his security from inflicting upon insolence the punishment which an angry temper would suggest.

Finally, Taney's own words, as quoted after his death in a letter written to Tyler from Taney's old family priest Father John McElroy, serve as a testament to the central role of his Catholic faith in his life. Father McElroy was with Taney a few days after his wife's death, when a friend came to offer the Chief Justice a carriage ride in the country to help relieve his grief. Taney declined. He then said this to Father McElroy:

> The truth is, Father, that I have resolved that my first visit should be to the Cathedral, to invoke strength and grace from God, to be resigned to His holy will, by approaching the altar and receiving holy communion.

Chief Justice of the United States Supreme Court

Roger Taney was nominated by President Jackson to be Chief Justice of the United States on December 28, 1835, succeeding the great John Marshall who had died. There was opposition in the Senate — one argument against him was that as a Catholic he would be dominated by the pope — but on March 15, 1836, Taney was confirmed by a vote of 29 to 15. He was two days short of his fifty-ninth birthday on that day.

A detailed study of the major opinions Taney authored or joined during his twenty-eight years on the Supreme Court is not possible here. A few of the major ones will be briefly considered and some general statements made about the legal and political philosophy expressed in his opinions and the manner in which he directed the Court. Then, a close look will be given to the *Dred Scott* decision and Taney's personal views on slavery.

Taney presided over the Supreme Court at a time when it no longer generally spoke as a corporate body, united behind the Chief Justice, as it had for most of Marshall's career. While, for the most part, it was not badly divided — except on some major cases like the *License Cases* and the *Passenger Cases*, discussed below — there were now dissenting opinions. Most of the time,

Taney was the leader of the Court, having written about three hundred opinions, very few of which were in dissent. His intelligence and legal competence are seen by the fact that most of these dissents are now accepted as correct expressions of the law. The somewhat greater disunity of the Court under Taney was due, most basically, to the heightened partisan conflicts in American politics generally. It was also due to the fact that, socially, the members of the Court, even while mostly still living together during term in Washington, began to go their separate ways more, and the fact that Taney, while a firm and strong man, did not have the dominating personality of a Marshall.

Taney's performance on the Court can best be appreciated by a speech made about him by his colleague, Justice Benjamin R. Curtis, after Taney's death. He told of how Taney:

> could ... state the facts of a voluminous and complicated case ... with extraordinary accuracy ... clearness and skill ... His mind was thoroughly imbued with the rules of the common law and of equity law ... His skill in applying it was of the highest order. His power of subtle analysis exceeded that of any man I ever knew ... but ... it was balanced and checked by excellent common sense and by great experience in practical business, both public and private ... The Chief Justice made himself entirely familiar with the rules of practice of the Court and the circumstances out of which they had arisen. He had a natural aptitude to understand and, so far as was needed, to reform the system. It was almost a necessity of his character to have it practically complete. It *was* a necessity of his character to administer it with unyielding firmness.

Charles River Bridge v. Warren Bridge was the first historic decision made by the Taney Court. Taney wrote the opinion which was handed down in February 1837. This decision upheld the action of the Massachusetts legislature of chartering a new toll bridge, owned by the Warren Bridge Company, over the Charles River at Boston in 1828. In 1785, the Charles River Bridge Company had been given the right to construct a toll bridge in the same area and this had replaced an exclusive ferry right held by Harvard College. The legislature permitted the latter bridge to be built so long as the company paid Harvard an annual payment during the course of the charter it granted to it. The plaintiff, the Charles River Bridge Company, had contended that giving the charter to Warren violated the previous charter and thereby violated the sanctity of contract guaranteed by the Constitution. Taney said in the opinion that the states had to have the freedom to act as the need arose in matters such as these for the welfare of the community. He also contended that to read the contract clause of the Constitution as prohibiting actions such as this would make it an obstacle to progress in transportation and the like.

The case of *New York v. Miln*, also decided in 1837, was another one of importance in the early Taney Court. He did not write the opinion, but assigned it to Justice Philip Barbour. It was another case permitting wide state latitude to make regulations in the interest of the public welfare (called the "police power" of the states). It sustained a New York law requiring the master of all incoming ships carrying passengers to report certain basic information about the passengers. The *License Cases* and the *Passenger Cases*, mentioned above and decided ten and twelve years later, respectively, divided on how far this idea of the "police power" could extend. The former upheld state licensing of liquor brought in from other states and the latter struck down state head taxes on new immigrants from other countries. The Justices wrote six separate opinions in the *License Cases* and eight in the *Passenger Cases*. Taney wanted to uphold both statutes and thus favored broad state "police power" in both cases.

Another significant decision of the Taney Court was *Bank of Augusta v. Earle* in 1839. Taney authored the opinion in that case, which overturned the decision of his colleague, Justice John McKinley, when he was sitting on circuit, that corporations, being artificial creations of the state of their incorporation, had no power to do business outside their own states and so could not enforce contracts they had made or purchased in another state. Taney held that the acts of a corporation, despite its being an artificial creation, are valid when not prohibited by local law. A corporation, he said, is entitled by the law of comity — which prevails in all the states of the Union — to make contracts in any state and have them enforced and have access to courts throughout the Union. The decision gave corporations the right to operate nationwide and, according to Lewis, "furnished the groundwork on which American corporation law was to develop."

Another important case of the Taney Court, which the Chief Justice did not participate in because of illness, was *Louisville etc. R.R. Co. v. Letson* in 1844. It clarified a question left open by the *Bank of Augusta* decision by holding that for purposes of a lawsuit a corporation should be treated as if it were a citizen of the state of its incorporation. This gave corporations access to the federal courts under their diversity of citizenship jurisdiction.

In 1848, Taney wrote the Court's opinion in *Luther v. Borden*. This case arose out of a near state of insurrection in Rhode Island. An attempt was made, backed by armed force, to put a new constitution into effect in place of the royal charter the state had kept in force since colonial times. The old royal charter had aroused much ire because there was no provision for amendment, it gave the franchise to very few men, and it maintained substantial disparities of legislative representation among areas of the state. In the face of the feared insurrection the state legislature declared martial law. Under powers given them by this edict of martial law, the state's militia broke into the home of Luther, a supporter of the forces challenging the charter government. This led to the case that eventually wound up in the Supreme Court, where both sides hoped for a decision which would decide whether the royal charter or the new People's Constitution, adopted by a convention called by the insurrectionists, was to be the governing law of the state.

Taney did not oblige either side. He said that whether a state is going to change its form of government is its own decision, and whether it has actually decided to exercise that sovereign power is up to the political power, not the judicial, to decide. The Constitution gave this power to Congress, which by an act of 1795 had rested the power to make the decision as to the legitimate government of a state on the President. The Court stood united behind Taney on this point, but his unwillingness to pass judgment on the propriety of the breaking into Luther's home — which he apparently thought would mean the Court would have to indirectly address the charter government's legitimacy — resulted in a dissent by Justice Levi Woodbury. Woodbury said that the legislature had no authority to declare martial law.

Taney consistently favored the Court's steering clear of political questions, as seen further in his concurring opinion in *Rhode Island v. Massachusetts* (1845), when he sought to have the Court refuse jurisdiction over a state boundary dispute, in the *Wheeling Bridge Case*, in which in dissent he said Congress and not the Court had the authority under the commerce power to decide if a bridge built by Virginia over the Ohio River could be allowed to stand over Pennsylvania's objections, and in *Groves v. Slaughter* in which the Court sidestepped facing directly the question of whether Mississippi could bar the importation of slaves into the state. It is ironic that it was the Court's acting to decide a political question in the *Dred Scott* case which would tarnish Taney's judicial career.

In 1851, Taney authored the Court's opinion in the important *Genesee Chief* case, which extended the admiralty jurisdiction of the federal courts to inland waterways in the U.S. In the 1852 case of *Cooley v. Board of Wardens*, the Court achieved what Lewis calls "a satisfactory compromise between the Commerce Clause views of Marshall and Taney." Marshall's decisions had had the effect of concentrating the commerce power in the hands of Congress; Taney had stressed giving more freedom to the states, even while not undermining the precedents set in this area by Marshall. Taney's principle had generally been to let the states regulate commerce whether interstate or not, in the absence of Congressional legislation. Seeing the need for a modification of this position, and believing that there was a need to find more of a middle ground between his and Marshall's views, he assigned the *Cooley* opinion to Justice Benjamin R. Curtis. Curtis enunciated the following new rule in the opinion: matters in the realm of commerce which are by their nature national, or can feasibly be dealt with only by a uniform plan of regulation, can be regulated only by Congress, and matters which are essentially local, or demand different responses in different areas, may be regulated by the states in the absence of preemptive Congressional regulations.

One more case of Taney's deserves mention before our discussion of *Dred Scott*, even though it was decided a year after it. This is *Ableman v. Booth* (1859), which also involved the issue of slavery, although more fundamentally concerned state versus federal power and the preeminence of the Supreme Court over state judiciaries. The case emerged from the federal prosecution of abolitionist editor Sherman S. Booth of Wisconsin for rescuing Joshua Glover, a fugitive slave, from the custody of a U.S. Marshal who had apprehended him under the authority of the Fugitive Slave Law. The Wisconsin Supreme Court twice freed Booth from federal custody by writs of *habeas corpus* on the ground that the Fugitive Slave Law was unconstitutional. It went even further by refusing to cooperate with the attempt to appeal its actions to the U.S. Supreme Court. The Supreme Court historically has closed ranks when faced with actual or likely defiance of its institutional prerogatives. This was no exception. In a unanimous decision on March 7, 1859, the Court reversed the Wisconsin Supreme Court's two actions of ordering Booth's release. In the Court's opinion, which the eminent Supreme Court historian Charles Warren called the "most powerful of all his notable opinions," Taney wrote that ". . . No one will suppose that a Government which has now lasted nearly seventy years . . . could have lasted a single year . . . if offenses against its laws could not have been punished without the consent of the State in which the culprit was found . . ."

Some general conclusions can be made about Taney's judicial and political philosophy as expressed in his opinions. First, it is true, to some extent, that Taney was concerned about "states' rights." As indicated, however, he merely favored a position which would give the states the right to exercise their authority on matters such as commerce when the federal government chose not to exercise *its* authority. He did not dispute the need for nationalizing certain matters, including most questions of commerce. He simply modified and clarified the nationalizing decisions of the Marshall Court and even promoted further nationalization in some areas himself. One might say that he promoted "states' rights" by the fact that he took a liberal view of state "police power" to allow the states to pass much social legislation. This was occurring, however, at a time before the federal government was doing much of anything in this area. All in all, Taney's view here could be said to be a moderate and reasonable one.

Taney was sensitive to the need for constitutional flexibility to permit "progress" in the country to go forth, as witnessed in the *Charles River Bridge* decision. Certainly, as the Bank controversy attests, he had suspicions of concentrated wealth and power. He did not blindly condemn all wealth in the manner an ideologue, either Marxist or non-Marxist leftist, would today. Rather, he resisted it when he believed it was acting against the public good. Thus, he forcefully opposed the Bank, but did not oppose permitting greater prerogatives and rights for business corporations because the greater vigor they promised to bring to American commerce and industrialism promised to promote the public good. The Constitution was not clear on a question like this and so the Court was able to exercise some discretion. Taney elected to let public opinion and legislative wishes about progress for the nation hold sway.

Except for *Dred Scott*, Taney's deference to the political authorities was admirable, especially since it is not seen enough in courts today. He did this because he believed it was what the Constitution demanded and he had confidence that the people's chosen leaders could decide wisely.

Slavery, The Dred Scott Decision, and the War Between the States

On March 6, 1857, the Taney Court handed down its decision in *Dred Scott v. Sandford*. It was a decision which ultimately weakened the Supreme Court for a generation, indirectly led to the War Between the States, and left Roger Brooke Taney as a hated and vilified man for the rest of his life and with a permanent black mark in the history books.

The background to the *Dred Scott* case must briefly be discussed before the Court's decision can be considered. The first significant event affecting this case occurred almost a generation before the first judicial action involving it took place. This was the passage in Congress of the Missouri Compromise of 1820 which prohibited slavery in the part of the Louisiana Territory north of 36° 30'. Dred Scott, a black slave, was taken by his owner Dr. John Emerson to Fort Snelling, which was north of the 36° 30' point. Dr. Emerson died after returning to Missouri, his home, from Fort Snelling and left Scott to his wife Irene. Irene Emerson planned to move to Massachusetts. She could not take Scott and his family with her and, while still formally the owner, left him behind to be tended to by one Taylor Blow, son of his original owner. The litigation began in April 1846, when a lawyer learned of the situation and sued Mrs. Emerson for Scott's freedom. Mrs. Emerson won in the Missouri trial court, but a new trial was granted on a legal point. The Missouri Supreme Court affirmed this ruling calling for a new trial. The second trial resulted in a directed verdict for Scott, but this was reversed by the Missouri Supreme Court and sent back for yet another trial. In the meantime, Mrs. Emerson moved to Massachusetts, which meant diversity of citizenship and a removal of the case to federal court. One Edmund C. LaBeaume, a Blow in-law whom Scott was hired out to at court order for the duration of the litigation, sought out an anti-slavery lawyer and Mrs. Emerson, who was remarried to an abolitionist Massachusetts Congressman, turned Scott over to be the subject of an effort to bring the question of slavery in the territories to the Supreme Court. In the U.S. Circuit Court in Missouri in 1854, the judge ruled that Scott was still a slave. Fifteen days later, the Kansas-Nebraska Act, which repealed the Missouri Compromise and permitted inhabitants of the Western territories to vote whether they wanted slavery or not, was passed by Congress. Taylor Blow put up the costs to have the case brought to the Supreme Court. The real issue in the case was not really Scott's freedom, but the constitutionality of Congress' prohibiting slavery in the territories under the Missouri Compromise.

There was initially serious division on the Supreme Court about whether it even had jurisdiction to take the case. It was argued twice before the Justices. There was also sharp disagreement on whether the question of the Missouri Compromise should be considered. Initially, the Justices decided not to do so, then it became known that Justices Curtis and John McLean planned to write dissents going into some of the controversial issues the Court had hoped to sidestep, including this one. The other Justices, especially those from the South, resented this and voted also to consider the issue of the Missouri Compromise. Taney, apparently, had to be persuaded to follow this course of action. He did so, however, and wrote the Court's opinion.

There were several controversial points made by Taney in the opinion. First, he accepted the Missouri Supreme Court's holding that Scott was still a slave. Second, he held that, even if he were not presently a slave, as a descendant of slaves — and this, of course, applied to all blacks who were descended from slaves — he could not claim citizenship under the Constitution. Taney said this was simply because it is what the Framers of the Constitution intended. This was the result of the "state of public opinion" at that time about the black race both in America and throughout "the civilized and enlightened portions of the world." He continued:

> They had for more than a century before [the adoption of the Constitution] been regarded as beings of an inferior order, and altogether unfit to associate with the white race, either in social or political relations; and so far inferior, that they had no rights which the white man was bound to respect; and that the negro might justly and lawfully be reduced to slavery for his benefit.

Taney backed up this argument by pointing to the fact that all the states, North and South, practiced substantial discriminations even against free black men at the time of the Constitution's adoption. He went into examples at much length. All the states which had abolished slavery at that time denied blacks full equality with whites. Even if a free black had the status of a citizen of his state, it did not follow that he was a United States citizen. Congress, he said, itself had refused to recognize him as such, and refused to grant him equal status with the white man in several federal laws. In short, Taney believed his assertions to be on firm historical and legal ground.

Taney went on to address the matter of the constitutionality of the Missouri Compromise and whether Scott was emancipated since he was brought above the 36° 30' line by Dr. Emerson. The claim that Scott was free because of the Compromise was based on two points: first, the constitutional provision which gives Congress the authority "to dispose of and make all needful rules and regulations respecting the territory belonging to the United States," and second, a statement made by Chief Justice Marshall in his opinion in *American Insurance Co. v. Canter.* Taney dismissed both of these possible bases. The constitutional provision in question, he said, applied only to the territory within the original boundaries of the U.S., not to areas subsequently acquired, such as that which Scott was taken into (which had been acquired from France in the Louisiana Purchase). A close study of the language of the Constitution and of its historical background had convinced him of this. Taney claimed that the Marshall decision mentioned was misread by those putting it forth as a precedent. This case did not acknowledge in Congress any power over the rights of person or property; it did not give Congress the same power to abolish slavery in the territories that a state has to abolish it within its borders. Taney further emphasized that the Constitution clearly recognized slavery. Taney's decision was joined by six other Justices, although some wrote concurring opinions. Two Justices, Curtis and McLean, dissented.

The outcry against the *Dred Scott* decision was swift and fierce. Lewis tells us that Taney bore much of the attack, and explains the nature of it:

> Both because he was Chief Justice and because he had written the major opinion, Taney was singled out for special attack. His opinion was called false, prejudiced, feeble, lying, Jesuitical, and much else. The attacks took three principal forms: (1) that the decision was part of a pro-slavery conspiracy; (2) that is purported to decide issues not properly before the court; and (3) that Taney had deliberately sought to degrade Negroes.

We are not able to evaluate the constitutional or legal correctness of the decision here. The Court and Taney were attacked as being anti-Negro and, as regards Taney, this is what we must be concerned about because we are trying to evaluate him as a man and a statesman.

Taney's biographers contend that his opinion reflected his understanding of constitutional law. He made the assertions he did because he concluded that the legal and historical background could enable him to make no other, not because he was pro-slavery or anti-Negro. Certainly Taney made a good case for his position, if not in his opinion itself then in the unofficial supplement to it he prepared which was included as an "Appendix" to Tyler's "Memoir" of him. Let us consider some other facts that are known about his life to determine what his attitudes on blacks and slavery actually were.

I have already mentioned some incidents in his life which suggest a respect for the dignity of blacks. This is perhaps further indicated by the fact that Taney in Baltimore was legal counsel to an organization formed to help protect the liberty of free blacks, who were often kidnapped in northern or border states and taken to the South to be sold as slaves.

Taney had emancipated his own slaves, except for two elderly ones who would have been unable to care for themselves. He had special copies of a photograph taken of himself in his judicial robes in 1860 to give to his old black servants. He wrote on the pictures, "As a mark of my esteem, R.B. Taney." He once made a substantial loan to a free black man to enable him to purchase his wife's liberty. He once spoke in the Maryland senate against a proposal regarding the Missouri Compromise which was being pushed by slaveholders because he believed state legislatures did not have the authority to give instructions to members of Congress. Taney was a vice president of the American Colonization Society, organized by his brother-in-law Francis Scott Key to create a colony for free blacks in Liberia. In his argument to the jury in the *Gruber* case discussed above, he indicated the belief that slavery was inimical to the Declaration of Independence and referred to "the galling chain of slavery." All these facts paint a picture of a man considerably different from the individual referred to in *The Unjust Judge*, a vicious anonymous pamphlet about Taney published after his death, who, it claimed, "falls below the lowest standard of humanity, religion and law recognized among civilized men."

Still, even if Taney did not disdain blacks or extol slavery, one must legitimately wonder how Taney, as a supposedly devout Catholic, could write a major judicial opinion accepting the existence of slavery and seeming to give it a legal imprimatur. Should not one have put aside the legal precedents and cast a blow, with whatever force one's station would permit, against a terrible evil such as slavery? There are three reasons, I believe, why we cannot condemn Taney for this and why his action in *Dred Scott* cannot be so readily judged as immoral or unChristian. First, he did what he believed he had a duty to do: interpret the Constitution and apply the law as he could best discern it. A sense of duty was something that always characterized Taney's career and he could noi make an exception to this in *Dred Scott*. The need for the Christian public official to carry out his duties, even when they sometimes conflict with Christian principles, was stressed by so great a Christian writer as St. Augustine. Secondly, Taney, like Lincoln, genuinely believed that precipitantly ending slavery would cause a political convulsion in the Republic, and there is every reason to believe he was correct. The fact that slavery offended the principles of the Declaration of Independence had to be kept in mind, but political prudence required that it be tolerated for some time. And thirdly, the fact that slavery is a great evil and is prohibited by the natural law is not something which was readily apparent for most of human history and was not even certainly taught by his Church, the guardian and interpreter of the natural law. The content of the natural law remains almost entirely as it always has been, but it is only over time, as man has become more civilized and morally sophisticated, that he has been able to fathom certain aspects of it. This is the way it was with slavery. Statements had been made against it by eminent Catholic teachers and Churchmen over the centuries, but it had never authoritatively been taught as wrong by the Magisterium up to Taney's time. Taney lived at a time when the Church's teaching was only beginning to come down firmly against slavery.

Taney's remaining years were ones in which many viewed him as an infamous and even hated figure. He accepted this, however, with resignation — probably because of his faith. It did not cause him to become any less assertive in doing his judicial duty. The *Booth* case was yet to follow *Dred Scott*, and so was *Ex parte Merryman* (1862), in which he issued a writ of *habeas corpus*, ignored at President Lincoln's orders, to the military authorities controlling Maryland to secure the release of a man being held without trial for supposedly — it was quite questionable — treasonous activity, and also the *Prize Cases* (1863), which challenged Lincoln's authority to blockade Confederate ports in 1861 without Congressional sanction.

Even with all the vilification and unjust attacks he sustained in the final years before his death on October 12, 1864, it would have been possible for the fair-minded person to get a true assessment of both the *Dred Scott* decision and the man, Roger Brooke Taney. In the midst of the fire spewed forth by pro-abolitionist newspapers, a few organs of the press *did* analyze the case calmly, fairly, and dispassionately and realized exactly what Taney had done and why he did it. After his death, the greatest personal tributes were paid to Taney by his judicial colleagues, the men who, like Justice Curtis — a dissenter in *Dred Scott* — were with him most and knew him best. They tried to give the whole picture of Taney and knew that he should not be judged *just* by *Dred Scott*. In addition to Curtis' comments mentioned earlier, he stated this about Taney:

> So long as he lived, he preserved that quietness of temper and that consideration for the feelings and wishes of others which were as far as possible removed from weak and selfish querulousness ... The surpassing ability of the Chief Justice, and all his great qualities of character and mind, were more fully and constantly exhibited in the consultation-room ... than the public knew ... There, his dignity, his love of order, his gentleness, his caution, his accuracy, his discrimination, were of incalculable importance. The real intrinsic character of the tribunal was greatly influenced by

them; and always for the better ... He was as absolutely
free from the slightest trace of vanity and self-conceit as any
man I ever knew ... The preservation of the harmony of the
members of the Court, and of their good-will to himself, was
always in his mind.

Perhaps the best statement of the kind of man Taney really
was is that men who were once his greatest political enemies, like
Curtis, came later to speak highly of him, and that other men who
met him only after forming negative views of him from his
uncomplimentary popular political and judicial reputation
immediately saw the goodness in him. Examples of the latter
were Edward Bates, Lincoln's first Attorney General, who wrote
in his diary that Taney was "the last specimen within my
knowledge, of a graceful and polished old fashioned gentleman";
Samuel Freeman Miller, a Lincoln appointee to the Supreme
Court, who said that before coming to the Court he had "hated"
Taney for his actions both in the Bank controversy and the *Dred
Scott* case, but after serving with Taney said "I more than liked
him, I loved him" and of "that great good man, I stand always
ready to say that conscience was his guide and sense of duty his
principle"; and Ward Hill Lamon, whom Lincoln appointed U.S.
Marshal for the District of Columbia, who stated that Taney's
"gracious courtesy and kind consideration" always made him feel
that he "was a better man for being in his presence."

Roger Brooke Taney was not a man without faults, nor one
that did not make mistakes in either his personal or his public
life. Yet, as we look at the whole of his life and public career —
which certainly *must* be done if we are to make a truly objective
and accurate assessment — we must conclude that he was a great
jurist and eminent American statesman. He was also a good *man*.
Somehow we are led to believe that in both life and death, Roger
Brooke Taney pleased his God.

Bibliography

Lewis, Walker. *Without Fear or Favor: A Biography of Chief Justice Roger Brooke Taney.* Boston: Houghton Mifflin, 1965.

Palmer, Ben W. *Marshall and Taney: Statesmen of the Law.* N.Y.: Russell and Russell, 1966.

Schauinger, J. Herman. *Profiles in Action: Catholics in American Public Life.* (Chapter on "Roger B. Taney, Chief Justice.") Milwaukee: Bruce, 1966.

Swisher, Carl Brent. *Roger B. Taney.* Hamden, Conn.: Archon, 1961.

Tyler, Samuel. *Memoir of Roger Brooke Taney, Ll.D.* Baltimore: John Murphy & Co., 1872.

7

Orestes A. Brownson: American Catholic Political Thinker (1803-1876)

AMERICO D. LAPATI

Orestes Brownson stands as one of the most controversial religious, social, and political thinkers of the nineteenth century. His switches in religious affiliations and from radical to conservative views make him a unique thinker and one whose influence was upon many a major issue of his time. No matter what religious faith he was espousing, he always looked upon religion as a force to change society and not as something solely personal and private. Martin Marty aptly classifies him as a "public theologian," for Brownson's vision of reforming society had always to be complemented by political praxis. His conversion to Roman Catholicism at the age of forty-one brought on a theological serenity of mind and less radical and more sobering stances on social and political reform.

I

Orestes Augustus Brownson was born in 1803 in the frontier town of Stockbridge, Vermont, and he and his twin sister were the youngest of six children. The father's death caused Orestes to be placed at an early age under the care of an elderly couple steeped in New England Congregationalism. Brownson's childhood was characterized by a stern and severe morality, a religious environment of God-fearing and moral honesty and uprighteousness. Although he joined the Presbyterians at the age of nineteen — his first religious commitment — he left them less than two years later because of their morbid outlook and anguish produced by the Calvinist teaching of the total depravity of human nature and of predestination with possible eternal punishment.

Because of his search for religious truth, Brownson became attracted to Universalism, which, in contradistinction to Calvinism, denied eternal damnation and offered to all men an assurance of salvation. In 1826 he was accepted as a Universalist minister, and he had the additional duty of being editor of the *Gospel Advocate*, an influential semi-monthly Universalist journal. Since salvation stood uppermost in his religious aspirations, he had to ascertain beyond doubt the guarantee of its attainability. But he found that the texts teaching salvation in Sacred Scripture were employed with equal force by those who argued salvation and by those who argued damnation. Confronted with such a dilemma, Brownson felt forced to reject the Bible as a source of and as a clear guide to religious truth. He found himself a skeptic and began to question the very existence of God. In the novel, *Charles Elwood, or the Infidel Converted*, Brownson described his intellectual struggle with skepticism. Although he first wrote the book in 1834, he did not publish it until 1840; the book reflects, therefore, his thinking from late 1829 to the beginning of 1831.

II

For Brownson the year 1829 not only represents a revolt

against traditional Christianity but also marks the questioning of the social conditions of his day and the inability of society to cope with the attendant social problems generated by the Industrial Revolution. A meeting with the Scotswoman Frances Wright led Brownson into exploring the radical social and utopian ideas and experiments prevalent in the first half of the nineteenth century in the United States. Robert Owen, Albert Brisbane, Horace Greeley, George Rapp, John Humphrey Noyes, Adin Ballou, Joseph Smith, Brigham Young, George Ripley — all had inaugurated socialist communities throughout the country.

Peaceful withdrawal was not, however, regarded as the sole solution to the inequities brought about by industrialization. Americans were learning from the struggle that was taking place in England, where the working class had already begun to react to the laissez-faire economic philosophy of Adam Smith. The deplorable working conditions and treatment of workers provided data to support the radical socialist theses of Friedrich Engels' *Conditions of the Working Class in 1844* and of Karl Marx's *Das Kapital*. Economic discontent led laborers to seek to better their lot by political agitation, from which arose the English Chartist movement in 1838. Repercussions of this movement were felt in the United States, for workingmen saw in labor organizations a means to achieve their goals for social and economic reform. Workers were encouraged by the election of Andrew Jackson in 1828 as one who was regarded as a "son of the soil" and as a "man of the people." Hundreds of local trade societies were formed from 1825 to 1837. Workingmen's parties were to be found in almost all industrial cities.

At Wright's invitation, Brownson became a corresponding editor of the *Free Enquirer*, which she published with Robert Owen's son, Robert Dale. They united their efforts with the Workingmen's Party of New York to achieve the Owenite goals. The Owen major premise consisted in the belief that man was but a passive creature of the circumstances in which he found himself; a program of reform would seek to lift him above his unfortunate status. This was to be accomplished by a plan of "state guardianship" in the education for all children beginning with the age of two.

Wright and Brownson, however, failed in their efforts to influence the workingmen to accept Owen's ideas. Brownson had never wholly accepted the state-supported system of education; he looked upon it as an infringement of the role of the family in the rearing of children. He, therefore, severed his connection with the *Free Enquirer* and with the extreme radical views of Owen and Wright.

III

But Brownson never lost hope for effecting social reform. Convinced that moral reform was the basis for social reform, he assumed the role of an independent preacher in 1831 and a year later associated himself with the Unitarians. He also began the editing and publishing of the fortnightly journal, *The Philanthropist*. Skepticism, he had found, was too negative and destructive; the positive force of religion was needed to attain social progress.

Brownson's views on and his interest in social reform attracted the attention of his fellow Unitarian ministers, William Ellery Channing and George Ripley. At their suggestion he went to Boston in 1836 to evangelize the working classes. With a following assured, Brownson established the Society for Christian Union and Progress for Boston's workingmen. As a guide for this organization, he published *New Views of Christianity, Society and the Church* (1836). *New Views* became for Brownson a hope for offering a program of social progress based on religion. The significance of this work is that Brownson synthesized in it the views he had been mulling over in his mind for some time. Christianity was not to be a matter of concern for one day of the week only and for the world to come; instead, it was to be an integral part of man's day-to-day life on earth.

But Brownson found it necessary to abandon his approach to social reform by individual moral reform; for he saw that social conditions could influence moral behavior. It was useless to preach the power of prayer when the power to earn a living did not exist. Economic conditions brought on by the Panic of 1837 — the failure and suspension of banks, the closing of factories, and a depression putting many laborers out of work — convinced him that action was necessary. Identifying the Whigs as the party of the greedy plutocracy, he backed the Democratic Party as the laboring man's hope for social and economic progress.

To aid the Democrats in the presidential election of 1840, Brownson published in *The Boston Quarterly*, which he had begun editing in 1838, one of his most controversial essays, "The Laboring Classes." In strong, unequivocal language the essay chastised the lot that industrial capitalism had imposed on the workingman. Not even the injustices of slavery in the South could compare to those of the laborer in the North. Under the pretext of paying wages, the industrial capitalist assuaged his conscience for the deplorable working conditions of his "slaves."

Brownson's essay became a campaign issue in the election. The Whigs classified it as evidence of the socialist tendencies of the Democrats. The Democrats, in turn, staunchly disavowed its ideas and dismissed Brownson as in any way a spokesman of their party. Religious leaders and the periodicals of the day attacked Brownson's charges as exaggerations and his views as social radicalism, even calling him a Jacobin and an American Robespierre. When election day in November, 1840, gave victory to the Whig candidate, William H. Harrison, the results embittered Brownson, who had placed so much hope in the people. He lost faith in the people, who failed to demonstrate faith in their own party. How could he champion the cause of the people if the people themselves would not rally behind their own party?

IV

Because of his loss of faith in the people as their own rulers, Brownson began a reappraisal of the American democratic system of government and a formulation of his own political thought. His political writings, appearing first in the *Boston Quarterly Review*, showed a marked trend toward conservatism. Reflecting an Aristotelian influence, Brownson regarded government to be necessary as the custodian of the common good. Government was not a mere necessary evil to prevent the encroachment of one individual upon another or encroachment by various groups. Government's role was positive: to work for social progress, to maintain individual liberty, and to develop the manifold resources of a country for its people — ideas to be reshaped and enlarged upon years later in his *The American Republic*. Unlike his early religious and social thought, his political writings do not demonstrate the same radical tendencies, due most likely to the fact that he did not record in writing his thoughts on political philosophy while he was engaged in radical social movements.

But, for the time being, Brownson saw no place for himself in practical politics. Man could not decide what was good for himself; he belonged basically, by inheritance from Adam, to a race of sinners. It must take time for sinful creatures to see and choose the good. Instead, Brownson gave himself to the writing of *The Mediatorial Life of Jesus* in 1842, in which he reverts to the role of religion in man's life as a more dynamic and practical mode of perfecting society.

V

The establishment of Brook Farm in 1841 under the leadership of George Ripley provided Brownson with a quiet, happy retreat from the warring classes of society. Some of America's outstanding intellectuals of the nineteenth century were from time to time associated with the Transcendentalist and socialist community, with some of whom Brownson had occasion to rub elbows: Ralph Waldo Emerson, Theodore Parker, Bronson Alcott, William Ellery Channing, Henry David Thoreau, Margaret Fuller, Charles A. Dana, and George Bancroft.

While Brownson appeared to favor much of the social and intellectual camaraderie at Brook Farm, he was ill at ease with the Transcendentalism of his confreres. He was too realistic; the others, too idealistic. He saw man capable of sin; they looked upon man as sinless. He viewed religion as objective; they looked upon religion as an inward, subjective emotion. Being neither popular nor happy at Brook Farm, Brownson cut short his stay.

It was back to political theorizing and practical politics. He still had in mind the election of 1840 as he wrote. With loss of faith in the people he no longer accepted the democratic view expressed in the words, "the intelligence of the people." Nor could he see the future of freedom being secured through a greater extension of popular suffrage. He objected to the definition of democracy as the sovereignty of the people. The view that democracy is a form of government, he believes, is erroneous; democracy should be viewed as a principle rather than as a form. A true democrat seeks the freedom and progress of all men, which will not be secured by "loose radicalism" with regard to popular sovereignty and by the "demogogical boasts" of the virtue and intelligence of the people.

Because of these views Brownson was called undemocratic and was charged with forsaking the cause of the Democratic Party in working for the people's interests. He was even accused of turning Whig. Although the de-emphasis on the people's power in government was true, it was not a loss of faith in democratic institutions that characterized Brownson at this time. He preferred to regard democracy more as an end rather than as a means.

In 1843 he offered to the readers of the *Democratic Review* three articles on the "Origin and Ground of Government." His purpose was to present a scientific exposition of politics, a project he felt had not yet been adequately performed in the United States and that was a need for American politicians. In these essays he rejects the social compact theory of government, even though it may have been a theory of much influence upon the Founding Fathers. Such a theory, based on the assumption that government has and can have no just powers but those derived from the consent of the governed, resolves all government into self-government with no distinction between the governing and the governed, resulting in the situation where "the restrained is the restrainer, the guided is the guide, the directed director."

The concept of majority rule becomes another topic that he examines: can government acquire its power from the majority of the governed? If so, Brownson emphasized, the minority would remain at the mercy of the majority. Such a theory would destroy the foundation of morality, for it renders the distinction between right and wrong as not fixed and eternal but as arbitrary and variable, truly permitting "might to make right." Majority rule should be classified as a "mere *civil* regulation" and not as a natural right or as an ordinance of God.

For Brownson, all power is of God; and no government of mere human origin is or ever can be legitimate. Reasoning from the principle of Christian philosophy, he argues that all being must have its origin in a first being, which is called God, the source of all being. From man's freedom given to him by God, man makes the practical arrangements determining his civil rulers, and this choice of man is an expression of the divine will. Brownson's thinking as to the origin of government is a *via media* between the divine right of kings and the popular-sovereignty theories. He actually proposes a theocratic-democratic position, for he acknowledges the divine origin of government with rulers chosen by the free will of man. But such a notion of the origin of government is not Brownson's alone. The historian Bancroft so viewed it also, for he defined democracy as "eternal justice ruling through the people."

Brownson prefers to classify the American form of government as a constitutional republic rather than as a representative democracy. In a democracy the majority can enact any law it deems expedient for its own interests, but in a constitutional republic the majority is held in check by the constitution representing the will of the people as a whole. Guaranteed in this constitution are the equal rights of all citizens as God has bestowed them upon man, and these a majority of citizens, however large, can never take away.

In setting forth the American government as a constitutional republic, Brownson actually reiterated the views of *The Federalist Papers.* He may have been on the side of political orthodoxy, but his readers were under the impression that he nurtured undemocratic ideas. The editor of the *Democratic Review,* J. L. O'Sullivan, prefaced one of Brownson's articles with an apology for such views on the role of the people in the American government. Brownson's analysis of the evils in American society led to his preferring some of the features of feudalism to industrial capitalism. Readers of his articles sent complaints to the editor inquiring about Brownson's verbosity and rather perplexing reasoning. Rising disapproval of the articles on government led O'Sullivan to request Brownson's withdrawing his services from the periodical and to disassociate himself from any of Brownson's views.

Withdrawing from the *Democratic Review* afforded Brownson the opportunity to clarify his stand in practical politics. He could more easily align himself now with the Southern Democrats instead of with the Northern Democrats. His admiration for Calhoun's political thought was to be extended to the putting of these ideas into the realm of practical politics. In October, 1841, Calhoun had suggested to Brownson his interest in the presidential nomination of 1844. An offer to edit a pro-Calhoun paper in New York in 1843 was made but later revoked because of lack of funds. Not having much regard for Van Buren who had charged that his essays on "The Laboring Classes" were a principal cause of his defeat in 1840, Brownson set out to oppose him. But again Brownson had to chalk up a defeat in practical politics. To his dismay Calhoun asked to be withdrawn from the race for the presidential nomination at the convention. Brownson did find occasion to rejoice when the Democrats rejected Van Buren and nominated instead James K. Polk. Although backing Polk, he took issue with him on the matter of the tariff because he felt the Democratic position discriminated in favor of home industry and so, in lessening the ability of the foreigner to sell to us, it likewise lessened his ability to buy from us. He nevertheless rejoiced in Polk's election victory and desired that his disagreement on the tariff issue not be taken as a sign of his dissenting from the Democrats and turning Whig but of his being no slavish adherent to a party and free to stress principles rather than party.

In 1843 Brownson wrote a series of articles on "The Mission of Jesus" for the weekly journal, *The Christian World*. These articles were significant in his thinking because in each article he arrived closer to the acceptance of Roman Catholicism, the religion he was to espouse until his death. But Brownson had not foreseen finding himself at the very doorsteps of Roman Catholicism when he began these articles. He even hesitated to acquiesce in the conclusions to which his arguments had led him. After considerable soul searching, he was formally received into the Catholic Church on October 20, 1844. While the doctrine of the mediatorial life of Christ and communion with it led Brownson to the door of the Catholic Church, it was belief in Christ's commission to the Church to teach all men and nations in matters affecting eternal salvation, which was made possible by participation in the living Body of Christ today, that actually became the rational basis for his complete acceptance.

Upon his conversion to Roman Catholicism, he founded *Brownson's Quarterly Review*, the immediate task of which became the defense of his new faith, especially by critical analyses of current Protestant theological writings. The intrepid defense and advocacy of Roman Catholicism in his articles brought him a well-cherished approbation from the American Catholic hierarchy in 1849 and also a special letter of encouragement from Pope Pius IX in 1854.

But Brownson was an independent thinker, without desire to please any individual or group. Love of truth was, as Isaac Hecker put it in *Catholic World* (November, 1887), his predominant passion. He would not sacrifice truth for popularity, financial gain, or a host of readers and followers. He loved an argument, not for the sake of argument, but because he could not be hypocritical and hold views contrary to his conception of truth. Even in his newly embraced religion he continued to be a controversial figure.

VI

Roman Catholicism may have assured Brownson a spiritual serenity in his search for religious truth. But he could not remain in smug complacency when men, living in the country he loved, were beset with socio-economic problems. Among the first problems to challenge his mind as a Roman Catholic was nativism. Alarmed at the rising influx of Catholic immigrants into this country, native-born Protestants organized themselves into societies to show concern about the new foreign influence. The Nativists found it difficult to accept the illiteracy, the poverty, and the dress of the immigrants.

In his writings Brownson sought to dispel the Nativist prejudice by declaring the patriotic sentiment of the newly arrived immigrants. Yet he did so with such a remarkable insight into the feelings of the Nativists that some of his co-religionists wondered on whose side he stood. Writing as a native-born American, Brownson saw no necessity for any movement against foreigners who desired to adopt a new country. Since its discovery America had been regarded as an asylum for the downtrodden and persecuted of the world. People from different lands and cultures had risen above purely accidental distinctions to join themselves together in a nation bound by the principle that all men were to be judged by their personal worth.

Brownson appealed to the Constitution to demonstrate the un-Americanism of the Nativists, for the Constitution not merely tolerates but also guarantees to all men the free exercise of their religion. He sought to allay the fears of the Nativists that Roman Catholics had a higher allegiance to a foreign power by pointing out the Catholic teaching on allegiance to civil authority and to country and the fact that a republic can stand only as it rests upon the virtues of the people. At the same time, however, he requested respect for native Americanism because the truest love of any man, after God, was for his country. He asked foreigners to appreciate the affection of Americans for their native land and the jealous attachment they had for its usages, manners, and customs. He warned of the immigrants' motives of personal advantage and gain in coming to this country; and, while they might wish to adhere to their own customs, it was for them to conform to Americans rather than for Americans to them. When these foreigners refused to accept American traditions and even spoke and wrote of undermining them, it was no wonder that they aroused justly the indignation and resentment of the native Americans. Brownson, therefore, censured Nativists for their close-minded bigotry and the immigrant Catholics for their foreign loyalties. The truth for him lay in a *via media*, at first unacceptable to either side; and, therefore, it left him without the sympathies from either side of the controversy.

Brownson's treatment of the Nativist controversy manifests a keen appreciation of the process of acculturation that has been taking place in our country since its founding. Acculturation cannot take place overnight; it is a gradual process. Acculturation seeks a blending of cultures, not a destruction of them. When assured of a blending, foreigners become more receptive to the process. Acculturation condones the holding onto cherished traditions even while it requires an allegiance to a new country, with its new customs, usages, and manners. Unity in diversity has been an ideal of American democratic life, and Brownson stands as one of those Americans who, in the nineteenth century at a crucial point of the country's population expansion, contributed to the process of acculturation of foreign Catholics into the country of their adoption.

VII

Brownson enjoyed no reputation for being on the side of the majority on many issues. Particularly in regard to states' rights and to slavery he held positions unexpected of a Northerner. Noticing a common lot between the helplessness of the Northern workingman at the mercy of the industrial capitalist and the Southern cottonpicker at the hands of the plantation owner, Brownson adopted more of the views of a Southerner than of a Northerner. He advised the Abolitionists to attend to their obligation of first cleaning up their own homes in the North before casting the stone of guilt at Southerners; for Brownson made no distinction between the evils of industrial capitalism and those of slavery.

In 1847 Brownson maintained that slavery was a matter for each state to decide and not a concern of the federal government. A new state seeking admission into the Union should not, therefore, be refused admittance because it believed in slavery, inasmuch as states presently members had such a right. He found such a justification in the states' rights theory expounded by John C. Calhoun in the *Disquisition on Government*. In typical Brownsonian fashion he stood alone among his fellow New Englanders in support of Calhoun's doctrine. It was a logical step to proceed to the defense of slavery, as he did, from the consideration of the economic interests of the states, in which the South found a strong argument to support slavery as an economic institution required for its very survival.

When slavery became a national problem to the point of Civil War, Brownson had to modify his position. He did not think that the South would ever secede from the Union and engage in war. Still preferring slavery to be decided on a local level with efforts for emancipation on a gradual scale, he now called for the preservation of the Union and for the defeat of the South. Yet, while defending the Union's cause in the war, he clearly pointed out that the Civil War should not be considered a war against Southern society and the Southern people; the war was only for a quick and successful preservation of the Union. Having shown sympathy for both sides, Brownson could well assume the role of *entrepreneur* of reconciliation between the North and the South — one of the main tasks when he came to write *The American Republic*.

VIII

Brownson's relations with his fellow Catholics were frequently controversial. His appeal to their making the Church more American and less Irish — believing that the progress and influence of the Catholic Church depended on its ability to acclimate itself to a new culture — brought denouncement for enkindling anti-Irish sentiment. His qualified endorsement of Catholic parochial schools enraged the American hierarchy; for Brownson urged parents to send their children to public schools when these were evidently superior to parochial schools, which too frequently employed foreigners or those of foreign sympathies and connections. His support of Catholic schools depended on their assuming a new perspective: training Catholic youths to meet the needs of a pluralistic society in which they lived. Brownson at this point would have taken pride in reading the University of Notre Dame Report, "Catholic Schools in Action" (1966), which stated that the Catholic schools, founded to preserve European customs and religion in an Anglo-Saxon and Protestant culture, have become in many ways more American than Catholic.

On one issue, the relationship of the spiritual to the temporal, Brownson engendered the most pronounced controversy. The liberal revolutions of the mid-nineteenth century gave Brownson much concern. Too many Americans, including Catholics, were extending their sympathies for the success of these revolutions, and these Americans failed, he thought, to realize that, although fighting under the banner of republicanism, the leaders were infidels seeking to destroy the influence of the Church and the papacy as part of the conservative remnants of European politics. He sought to warn of the rising tide of political atheism which sought to divorce the state from morality and religion. The desire to have religion play a more prominent role in a nation's political life also necessitated Brownson's writing on the proper relationship between the temporal and spiritual powers.

In five successive issues of his *Quarterly Review* in 1853 he offered views on these powers. Both powers received their authority from God, for God is the universal Lord, the sovereign King. The sovereign in all things and over all, God has made his law as universal as his dominion and providence. To Christ, God gave all power in heaven and on earth; and, as God Incarnate, He rules with all power and law. Christ, furthermore, established the Roman Catholic Church as the depositary, the guardian, and the judge of his law; and to its apostles and their successors has been given the divine authority to teach this sovereign law to all nations and also to teach them to observe its commandments.

Christian political philosophers had often declared the supremacy of the Church in spiritual matters, but they extended supremacy in temporal matters to the states, with the Church having a voice in temporal matters that in some way affects man's

spiritual concerns and the rights of the Church. Brownson,
however, gave the Church a supremacy in all matters. He was
convinced that he did not enunciate any new theory of Church
and state, as Pope Gregory VII in the eleventh century
considered it his duty to judge the activities of the secular power,
refusing the emperor's crown to Prince Henry IV of Germany
because of his practice of lay investiture. What Brownson forgot,
however, is that this notion of Gregory VII was a theory and not a
dogma of the Church, that it was expressed at the height of the
feudal Middle Ages to a united Christendom and not to a
pluralistic society as existed in the United States, and that this
was the crown of the Holy Roman Empire — a purely papal
creation, and not a nation-state. But Brownson insisted that the
spiritual order is supreme and, therefore, should prescribe the
law for the temporal. Protestantism receives his condemnation
for compromising between the two orders, a compromise that
eventually resulted in the total sacrifice of the spiritual and the
total supremacy of the temporal.

Brownson claims that subjects owe allegiance to their
legitimate civil rulers. To refuse to obey them or to resist their
authority are matters of serious sin against God; for, according to
the divine origin of power, there is no authority unless from God
and civil rulers rule by divine authority in temporal matters. But
as the temporal is subordinate to the spiritual, the spiritual power
determines the legitimate rulers and renders judgment on
matters of obedience to civil authority. Having reached a point
of obsession with his views on the supremacy of the spiritual over
the temporal, Brownson went on to attribute to the Pope the
power of deposing secular princes. He did not, however, claim
that the deposing power of the Pope could be applied to the
United States. As a matter of fact, he would reject its use in any
modern state since such a doctrine could be applied only if a
state were thoroughly Catholic. But in theory, as deduction from
the supremacy of the spiritual, he maintained that the Pope could
make a juridical declaration stating that a secular prince had

forfeited his rights to rule by acts of tyranny.

The bold assertions made by Brownson on the spiritual and temporal orders aroused much indignation on the part of both Catholics and non-Catholics. The criticisms ranged from "importune" to "un-American." The Know Nothings found in his stand one of their strongest arguments against the foreign Catholics: allegiance and obedience to the Pope in Rome preceded their loyalty to the United States. The pen of America's most forceful writer of the time provided fuel for the raging fire of bigotry. Members of the Catholic hierarchy were no less indignant in their criticism of Brownson's views. They had, furthermore, questioned his views on Nativism, even looking upon them as anti-Irish; they doubted whether the converted Catholic supported their stand on parochial schools. Several bishops publicly denounced him, withdrew their support of his *Quarterly Review*, and claimed that he was no longer to be considered a spokesman for Catholicism.

Since Brownson refused to submit to the wishes of the American bishops for a halt and even a recantation of his obnoxious views, the expected action took place. He was denounced to the Prefect of the Congregation of the Propaganda in Rome. Brownson was able to successfully defend and explain his views to Rome, and the failure of his enemies to secure condemnation only served to intensify his independence. But Rome was not among the paying subscribers to his *Quarterly Review*, and with the loss of prestige in the United States brought on by the attacks of the hierarchy, he discontinued publication in October, 1864.

IX

Freed from the necessity of meeting journal deadlines, and the preoccupation with sundry controversial subjects, Brownson now had an opportunity he had hardly ever had in his busy journalistic career. Time for more serious and profound reflection was available, and he employed this newly found leisure in the writing of *The American Republic*.

Dedicated to George Bancroft "as a sort of public atonement" for the harsh criticism made of earlier historical writings, *The American Republic* is an exposition of Brownson's political thought. Although the topics of the nature, necessity, extent, authority, origin, ground, and constitution of government, and the unity, nationality, tendencies, and destiny of the American republic had been discussed in previous writings, the work is the author's most complete and systematic, as well as his most developed thinking about the nature of politics.

Brownson considered it a necessity for a young nation to examine and realize its mission and destiny. Having adopted a constitution with no prototype in any prior constitution, he called for a profound study of its principles to demonstrate its contribution to political science. He pointed out that, while it retained the advantages of constitutions already adopted, it was unlike any of them and secured advantages which none of these did, or could, possess. Of particular importance was such a study in the light of the successful maintenance of the American system after the secession of the Southern states and the Civil War.

Although Brownson claimed that he did not take "bodily" from any of his previous essays on government, he reiterated many of his former views. He reasserted the divine origin of government, with rulers holding their political authority from God through the natural law. The people, moreover, had the right to set up their own constitution; and they also enjoyed the incontestable right to change their form of government, its magistrates, or its representatives. Granted that majorities determined a form of government and its constitution, the rights of minorities were never taken away; for minorities possessed inalienable rights by virtue of human nature antecedent to any constitutional document. These notions of government Brownson classified as basic in the American form of government.

The doctrine of state sovereignty, which Brownson held and defended from 1828 to 1861, was now rejected. Reasoning from the principles of government that he advocated, he concluded that God, operating through historical facts, constituted the American people as one political or sovereign people, existing and acting in particular communities called states. This one people organized as states met in convention, framed and established the constitution of government, or instituted a general government in the place of the Continental Congress. The same people, moreover, in respective states, met in convention in each state to frame and establish a particular government for each state individually, which — in union with the general government — constituted the complete and supreme government within the states. The general or federal government, in union with all the particular governments, constituted the complete and supreme government of the nation or whole country.

The answer to two basic questions determined whether one accepted or rejected the States' rights theory. Was United States politically one people, nation, state, or republic — or is it comprised of independent sovereign states united in close and intimate alliance, league, or confederation by a mutual pact or agreement? Were the people of the United States who ordained and established the written constitution one people, or were they not? Reaffirming that the people of the United States acted as one when adopting a federal constitution and that they adopted respective state constitutions as subordinate to the Federal Constitution, Brownson became a firm believer in a strong national government. He did not deny the states their own rights, since he upheld the Tenth Amendment's assurance of States' rights; but he forcefully declared the common good of any one state as subordinate to the common good of the nation.

The profundity and brilliance of Brownson's thinking reached its height in his analysis of the political and religious destiny of America. The special mission of the United States was to continue and complete the Greco-Roman civilization in the political order. On this point, he demonstrated that he was no disdainer of the past but that he wished America to retain all the good in the past as a steppingstone to progress in the future. Although he recognized republican elements in Roman government, he pointed out the great error of the Romans: denial or ignorance of the unity of the human race, as well as of the unity of God. Their sustaining a privileged class and their regarding power as an attribute of birth and of private wealth set limits upon the genuine equality of all men. The French and the English improved on the Roman concept of equality, but the former tended to socialism and the latter to pure individualism. The United States had more happily blended the division of powers with recognition of the rights of individuals; moreover, the power of the government on both national and state levels protected these rights and subordinated them to the common good of the people of the whole nation. The continuance of progress in the American democratic system of the balance of equal individual rights and of the powers of government was America's special political mission to the world.

Brownson's view of the role of the United States in world politics had the power of prophecy. To the United States would belong the hegemony of the Old World and of having a voice in adjusting the balance of power in Europe. To accomplish this role, the United States needed a great military and naval power. Military preparedness, he insisted, could serve as deterrent to war.

As for the religious destiny of the United States, Brownson sought neither to create a new religion nor found a new church. He would have religion stand above and independent of the state, with neither the state absorbing the Church nor the Church absorbing the state. Both Church and state were to move freely according to their own natures and proper spheres. Although externally they might be governing bodies, both Church and state were united in the interior principle which granted them vitality and force so that each could fulfill its respective mission. Brownson gave full recognition to the fact that the United States was a pluralistic society, that "false religions are legally as free as the true religion." An established or preferred religion would have no place in American democratic society; furthermore, having one would contradict the very nature of the independence of religion and the state, and would result in making religion a civil institution.

Brownson had high praise for the framework in which the Catholic Church could perform its religious mission in this country. Without any intervention or mediation of the state, the Church enjoyed freedom to act according to her own constitution and laws, and she exercised her own discipline on her own spiritual subjects. Brownson had now come to reason like most of his fellow Catholics in the United States. He discarded his old views on the supremacy of the spiritual over the temporal. Had he been less belligerent and adamant in his previous views regarding the relation of Church and state in this country, *The American Republic* would have had a much wider audience. As it was his fear of the book's being "neglected" was justified. If readers, however, could have forgotten Brownson's previous rashness, they would have found in *The American Republic* a political testament of profound thought on both the political and religious mission of American Catholics, and a contribution to a better understanding of America's great experiment in political thinking. If *The Federalist Papers* of Madison, Hamilton, and Jay can be considered among the best of philosophical explanations on the formation of the American form of government, Brownson's *The American Republic* ought to enjoy a similar evaluation as a philosophical exposition of the union restored after the Civil War.

X

After the suspension of the *Quarterly* in 1864, Brownson was left without a publication of his own to express his views. But a number of influential Catholics still saw in him a staunch advocate of the faith and a writer of extraordinary talent. Father Edward Sorin, founder of the University of Notre Dame, established the *Ave Maria* magazine in 1865 to extend devotion to the Blessed Virgin Mary as Mother of Christ. In 1866 Brownson wrote a series on the moral and social influence of devotion to Mary. The *Catholic World*, which also began publication in 1865, requested his services. Its editor-in-chief, Isaac Hecker, a convert to Catholicism, had been a friend of Brownson for many years. Translating articles from foreign languages at first constituted most of Brownson's work for this magazine, but he later wrote articles more conciliatory in tone than those which had been written before the suspension of the *Quarterly*. He also published articles in the New York *Tablet*; in these he modified earlier views on the ineffectiveness of Catholic education to train for American Catholic leadership and the supremacy of the spiritual over the temporal. These modified views found ready acceptance by the Catholic hierarchy, clergy, and laity.

Independent of mind as he was, Brownson naturally preferred being his own editor instead of a contributor. He subsequently revived the *Quarterly* in 1873 and continued it in a less belligerent tone for three years until November, 1875. Poor health forced him to relinquish its publication. He died on April 17, 1876.

XI

Throughout his life, but most especially after his conversion to Roman Catholicism, Brownson found it difficult to understand why so many questioned his logic and sincerity. In 1854 he wrote

The Spirit-Rapper: An Autobiography, in which he portrayed his reactions to misunderstandings of his motives. He personified in the characters of this novel many of the acquaintances of his life, among whom were Fanny Wright, Emerson, Alcott and Theodore Parker. However, the book was not a serious one, and it is in no way a delineation of his life and thought. Although expecting derision for his notion of spirit-rapping, Brownson found an explanation for his failures and misunderstandings. Mingled with the imaginative tales that he related was the strong conviction that Satan had sought to thwart his sincere efforts toward improving the lot of his fellow man.

The Convert; or Leaves from My Experience is Brownson's autobiography. Written in 1857, the book traces his religious experiences to his admission into the Roman Catholic Church. With his usual candor and intellectual honesty, he depicts the various stages in the development of his religious thought and a disavowal of the radical social tendencies that characterized his earlier life. But neither autobiography won for Brownson the acceptance and approval which he sought.

It has remained for the twentieth century to see Brownson in a more favorable light. His views and incessant pursuit of truth have attracted the attention of numerous scholars, both Catholic and non-Catholic. Not surrounded by the passions of those living in the nineteenth century, present-day scholars, although not necessarily in agreement with all that Brownson wrote, have paid respect to the force of his logic, the power of his intellectual analysis, his love for independence of thought, and the sincerity by which he sought objective truth. Roman Catholics can well look upon him as the intellectual layman *par excellence* of the nineteenth century. His place in history can best be described by Arthur Schlesinger, Jr., known for his scholarly study of Brownson, as a writer and thinker who is "vigorously alive as a figure in American intellectual history."

Bibliography

Brownson, Henry F. *Life of Orestes Brownson.* 3 vols. Detroit: Brownson, 1898-1901.

—————, Ed. *The Works of Orestes Brownson.* 20 vols. Detroit: Nourse, 1182-1907.

Gilhooley, Leonard. *Contradiction and Dilemma: Orestes Brownson and the American Idea.* New York: Fordham University Press, 1972.

—————, Ed. *No Divided Allegiance: Essays in Brownson's Thought.* New York: Fordham University Press, 1980.

Lapati, Americo D. *Orestes A. Brownson.* New York: Twayne, 1965.

Marshall, Hugh. *Orestes Brownson and the American Republic: An Historical Perspective.* Washington, D.C.: The Catholic University of America Press, 1971.

Maynard, Theodore. *Orestes Brownson: Yankee, Radical, Catholic.* New York: Macmillan, 1943.

Michel, Virgil G. *The Critical Principles of Orestes A. Brownson.* Washington, D.C.: The Catholic University of America, 1918.

Raemers, Sidney A. *America's Foremost Philosopher.* Washington, D.C.: The Catholic University of America Press, 1931.

Roemer, Lawrence. *Brownson on Democracy and the Trend toward Socialism.* New York: Philosophical Library, 1953.

Ryan, Thomas R. *Orestes A. Brownson: A Definitive Biography.* Huntington, Ind.: Our Sunday Visitor Press, 1976.

—————. *The Sailor's Snug Harbor.* Westminster, Md.: Newman Press, 1952.

Schlesinger, Arthur M., Jr. *Orestes A. Brownson: A Pilgrim's Progress.* Boston: Little, Brown, 1939.

Sveino, Per. *Orestes A. Brownson's Road to Catholicism.* New York: Humanities Press, 1970.

8

Peter Hardeman Burnett:
Pioneer and Politician (1807-1895)

STUART GUDOWITZ

During his long life, Peter Hardeman Burnett was many things: clerk, lawyer, businessman, banker, pioneer, judge, legislator, and the first governor of California. Though a relatively minor political figure, a study of him is not without interest for he was directly involved in two of the major events in nineteenth century America: the race question and the settlement of the western frontier.

Born on November 15, 1807 into a Baptist family, Burnett grew up in Tennessee and Missouri. His father, George, was a carpenter and farmer. At the age of nineteen, Burnett returned to Tennessee and clerked first at a hotel, then at a store. He married Harriet Rogers, a woman whom he described in his autobiography, *Recollections of an Old Pioneer*, written in 1880, thus: "a religious girl ... My wife was never noisy, fanatical, or wildly enthusiastic in her religious feelings, but she was *very firm*." He entered into business for himself in Tennessee and also in Missouri to which he later returned, amassing a rather large amount of debt. In his *Recollections*, Burnett relates two incidents from this time which illustrate the strictness and rectitude of his character. Both occurred in Tennessee. First, while selling whisky at his store, he found that he had acquired quite a taste for it, partaking of it, "in the morning and occasionally during the day." Concerned that his drinking might get out of hand, he, "soon determined that I would abstain entirely, which has been my general practice. As I do everything with all my might, I became satisfied that, if I indulged at all, I would be very apt to do some tall drinking." The second example occurred in 1830 when Burnett discovered that his store was being burglarized by a shutter being forced. He stayed up one night in the store to catch the thief, but fell asleep. He then rigged a shot gun aimed at the shutter so that, when the shutter was forced, the trigger would go off. In this way the thief was shot dead. It turned out to be a slave. Burnett, upon discovering the body, reported the incident and, though told he was not required to offer evidence that would tend to incriminate him, Burnett, as a witness at the inquest, told everything. He wound up not being prosecuted nor sued by the slave's owner. Burnett writes in his *Recollections*, "... in afterlife, I have deeply regretted the act; and, the older I become, the more I could wish it had never occurred ... I am hard to excite, but when fully aroused my natural feelings are desperate. But, thank God, through his mercy, the idea of shedding human blood is now terrible to me. I would rather bear almost any injury than take human life."

Burnett did not have very much formal education, but he loved to read. Eventually he studied law and began to practice in Missouri in 1839. In one case he was an attorney for Mormons charged with robbery, arson, and treason. He served as a prosecuting attorney from 1840 to 1842. In 1843, he joined a wagon train bound for Oregon. He did this with the permission of his creditors in the hopes that he could earn enough money in the west to pay off his debts. He was also concerned for his ill wife and the bad effect the climate was having on her.

Shortly after arriving in Oregon, Burnett became active in local politics, becoming a member of the Legislative Committee in 1844, a judge of the Supreme Court in 1845, and a member of the territorial legislature in 1848. It was in Oregon that Burnett entered the Catholic Church. Burnett had fallen away from Christianity in his youth, but returned via the Protestant denomination, the Disciples of Christ, also known as the Campbellites. Of this process, Burnett wrote, "My own observations of men and things, as well as the arguments of others, at length satisfied me that the system was divine, and I at once acted upon my convictions and joined myself to the Disciples in 1840." Four years later, Burnett came across a published debate between Campbell and Bishop Purcell which impressed him with how much there was to be said in defense of Catholicism. He decided "to examine the question between Catholics and Protestants thoroughly ... I procured all the works on both sides within my reach, and examined them alternately side by side ... After an impartial and calm investigation, I became fully convinced of the Catholic theory ..." He converted in June, 1846. His two apologetics books, *The Path Which Led a Protestant Lawyer to the Catholic Church* (1860) and *Reasons Why We Should Believe in God, Love God and Obey God* (1884) are certainly lawyerly in their considerations of various issues, and prolix. But it would be a mistake to think of Burnett's faith as simply a coolly rational affair. Near the end of the latter book, he writes, "I know that my religion has been the source of the greatest happiness to me in years that have fled, and that it is still dearer to me now, and I believe will so continue to the end of my journey. Oh! let me live the life and let me die the death of the Christians."

Still concerned about his indebtedness, he went off to the gold mines of California in 1848, not staying in the mines very long before he became an attorney and agent for the Sutter family. Once again, he became involved in local government and politics, serving as a judge on California's superior tribunal in 1849 and was elected governor in the November 13th elections of that year by a wide margin. He resigned on January 9, 1851 and returned to the practice of law, before the news of the admission of California to the union had been received. He was appointed to fill a vacant position on the state supreme court in early 1857 and served until October, 1858. Later he founded with others, the Pacific Bank of San Francisco, of which he served as president from 1863 to 1880. He died in San Francisco on May 17, 1895.

In both Oregon and California, Peter Burnett was involved in the establishment of government, the establishment of each being an object of controversy. One writer, David Lavender, goes so far as to accuse Burnett of encouraging people to go west in order to create his own political constituency. However that may be, it is a fact that Burnett was intimately involved in the Oregon Legislative Committee, consisting of nine members, when there was still no settlement between the U.S. and Britain in regards to Oregon. Burnett, in fact, at first held the opinion that Oregonians had no right to form a provisional government, but changed his mind. In his *Recollections* he states, "Communities, as well as individuals, have the natural right of self-defense; and it is upon this ground that the right to institute governments among men must ultimately rest. This right of self-preservation is bestowed upon man by his Creator . . . We also found, by actual experiment, that some political government was a *necessity* . . . Without any law but that of individual self-defense, we found it impossible to get along in peace." Of this provisional government, Lavender writes, "In some respects it was . . . astounding . . . While international diplomats exchanged stiff notes, while chauvinists in the United States Congress and the British House of Commons hurled inflammatory defiances, the men of Oregon, ignored by their governments, worked out a peaceable solution . . . It might have been chaos. Instead it turned out to be an order that was able to function, without sanction or money or power, until a stronger government finally got around to taking it over."

While on the Legislative Committee, Burnett introduced a bill which was enacted to prohibit slavery and the settling of free blacks in Oregon. (In his inaugural address as governor of California, Burnett proposed that free blacks be prohibited from settling there.) Burnett devotes quite a few pages in his *Recollections* defending himself in regard to this action. He says there that, for years before the bill, he had opposed slavery and that his reason for proposing prohibiting blacks from settling in Oregon was because the organic laws of Oregon, which were adopted in 1843, denied suffrage to blacks implicitly by limiting the vote to free white males. He argues that to disenfranchise a class of men in a democratic polity, and then to let them settle would provide a temptation for those with a vote to tyrranize the disenfranchised. (This, one presumes, is the same reason he opposed the settling of free blacks in California.) Burnett writes, "Had I foreseen the civil war, and the changes it has produced, I would not have supported such a measure. But at the time I did not suppose such changes could be brought about . . ."

Burnett also has a lot to say in his autobiography on the immigration of Chinese. He opposed Chinese laborers settling in the U.S. because he thought that should "the population of the globe . . . be left, like water, to find its own level," the west coast would eventually be dominated by Chinese and Caucasians would be excluded. He also lamented the fact that white boys would often terrorize Chinese. "The worst effect of the presence of the Chinese among us is the fact that it is making *tyrants and lawless ruffians of our boys.* It is true, the poor Chinamen suffer from this violence, but still their situation in California is better than their former half-starved condition at home." Thus he "opposed the residence of the Chinese among us, except for the purposes of trade." Only merchants would be allowed to reside in the U.S. but, again, he denies racial prejudice as his motivation: ". . . I am not conscious of prejudices against any race of man. I believe, with St. Paul, in the unity of the human race . . ." He does, in fact, express his opposition to expelling those already resident.

As in Oregon, Burnett was, in California, actively involved

in the establishment of a government without the permission of the U.S. Congress. As a result of the Mexican War, California, in May 1848, was ceded to the United States and a succession of military governors ruled, whose average term of service was six months. Congress adjourned in August without taking steps to establish a civilian government. This led to popular calls for the establishment of civilian rule culminating in a series of meetings beginning in late 1848. In fact, a Legislative Assembly of San Francisco was formed for that area and began functioning without the permission of the military government.

Those who opposed the formation of a provisional government without the permission of Congress, like military governor Bennet Riley, argued that, until Congress, which had the sole power to legislate, authorized the formation of a territorial government, the civil laws of Mexico still were in force and were to be administered by the military governor. Those who, like Burnett, favored the establishment of a temporary government by Californians, countered (to use Burnett's own summary from his *Recollections*):

> ... Mexican civil law [in California] had been ... superseded; that, the moment the treaty [ceding California to the United States] took effect, the Constitution ... [was] at once extended over the acquired territory; that the power to legislate was primarily vested in Congress, but that, while that body neglected and refused to exercise such power, it was no usurpation in the people of California to exercise it temporarily, and in strict subordination to the admitted right of Congress ... that nine tenths of the people of California were American citizens ... wholly unacquainted with the civil laws of Mexico, and with the language in which they were written and published; that ... it was not practical good sense or justice to require these nine tenths ... to learn the laws of Mexico for the short period to elapse before the new order of things was morally certain to take place ... and finally, that the temporary exercise of legislative power by the people of California was based upon the original and natural right of society to protect itself

by law, and that such exercise by our people was in no true
sense a violation of the law of nations . . .

In the above extended passage, we can easily discern, I
think, Burnett's combination of political theoretician and
practical politician.

Eventually, Governor Riley called a convention to write a
state constitution, which wound up prohibiting slavery and voting
down an attempt to prohibit free blacks from entering. The
constitution was eventually accepted by the U.S. Congress.
Burnett was elected the first governor in the same election at
which California ratified the constitution. On the question of
whether the legislature should begin to act immediately or should
refrain from enacting legislation until Congress acted to admit
California into the union, Burnett favored the former tack, and
the legislature concurred.

Later, as a judge of the California Supreme Court in 1858,
Burnett dealt directly with the issue of slavery. One Charles
Stovall brought his slave, Archy Lee, into California. Lee
eventually escaped. The anti-slavery provision in the California
constitution was clear and Burnett recognized that the law would
not allow the returning of Lee to Stovall. Yet he wrote in his
ruling, "But there are circumstances connected with this
particular case that may exempt him from the operation of the
rules we have laid down. This is the first case; and under these
circumstances we are not disposed to rigidly enforce the rule for
the first time. But in reference to all future cases, it is our
purpose to enforce the rules laid down strictly, according to their
true intent and spirit." (9 Cal. 147)

Thus, because Burnett believed that the petitioner Stovall
might have reason to believe that his slave would be returned to
him under California law — though this was, in fact, an
erroneous view — Burnett did not free the slave but ordered him
returned to Stovall, thus not "rigidly" enforcing the law.
According to Caughey and Hundley, a later court action set

Archy Lee free, but this writer has not been able to find any evidence of this later action, and they do not mention whether or not Burnett was involved in it.

This incident certainly can give us food for reflection, without, let us hope, our condemning Burnett himself. I do not think that his action in the court case discussed above, *Ex parte Archy*, need lead us to question his sincere opposition to slavery, but I think it can serve as a warning. Burnett stated that the law favored the freedom of the slave but ruled otherwise due to certain circumstances. One would think that a person, realizing the evil of American slavery, would go out of his way to do what he could to eliminate it in so far as he was able. As judge, and without violating the civil law in the least, he had a chance to free a slave, and did not do so. The warning to us, I suppose, is that we can easily become accustomed to the evils of our age, even when we recognize them as evils. We can cease to be shocked because the evil is endemic, and thus fail to truly recognize its enormity. In a similar way, Burnett, while in Oregon, worked for the prohibition of slavery there but also favored the prohibition of free blacks settling there, as has been discussed above. Burnett claims, and we have no reason to doubt him, that he did so for honorable reasons; and surely we can understand that politics is the art of the possible. But there is also the question of Christian witness, to which the Catholic is bound in whatever circumstances Providence places him. The question is (and I do not mean it to be rhetorical): Was it clear to Burnett's colleagues and constituency in Oregon that he thought the disenfranchisement of blacks to be wrong and that his proposal to prohibit them from settling in Oregon was his attempt to make the best of a bad situation? From the evidence I have available to me, it is impossible to say. But the broader lesson, I think, is that the Catholic must always try to judge the society in which he lives by the Gospel and try to act appropriately. It seems clear to me that Burnett's decision in *Ex parte Archy* was, to say the least, inadequate to the enormity of the evil of slavery. He seems to have let lesser considerations prevent him from dealing a blow against a very great evil. Then, too, the Catholic politician must not get so caught up in achieving what is practical that he neglects to bear witness. Any human institution in man's fallen state is bound to be, at best, a mixture of good and evil. The Catholic politician must be realistic about this and how much he can accomplish. But, as a Catholic, he must bear witness to the God of Light, in Whom there is no darkness.

After Burnett retired from public life, he wrote *The American Theory of Government Considered with Reference to the Present Crisis*, "the present crisis" being the war between the states. This is, again, a combination of political theory and practical politics. He was a man of great patriotic sentiments and certainly opposed the dissolution of the union, but he distinguished between loyalty to the country with an adherence to the constitutional regime. In fact, Burnett, who had been a Democrat and an admirer of Jefferson, came to regard Hamilton as the greatest of his generation. In his book, he proposed quite radical changes to the U.S. governmental system. He regarded the federal system's division of "that supreme element or principle which we call sovereignty" to be a grave mistake. He advocated that states, far from retaining powers not specifically delegated to the national government, should be "strictly subordinate corporations . . . only permitted to exercise such powers as may be allowed by Congress." He thought that the legislative actions of states should be revocable by Congress. He further advocated that the governors of the states be appointed by the president, with the advice and consent of the Senate, and hold their office at the president's pleasure. These governors were to have a qualified veto on acts of the state legislatures. As for the legislatures themselves, Burnett thought that the state senators should be elected by district for life and that members of the state houses of representatives should be elected by counties for four year terms. Clearly, Burnett was very concerned about the division of sovereignty between the national and state governments and was particularly concerned that the "dearest of all rights, the right of religious freedom, depends ... upon the will of each State, and not upon that of the whole." Nor did Burnett consider that the federal system was necessary for the preservation of liberty, for the powers delegated to the national government, even under his system, would be limited.

Another major weakness of the Constitution for Burnett was the short terms of office and the re-eligibility of incumbents. He wished to make public officials more independent and thus recommended that the president be elected for one twenty-year term and be ineligible to hold any other office. Burnett thought that a president elected for life might be more subject to assassination. He saw the Senate as the conservative branch of Congress and suggested that senators be chosen for life terms and be ineligible to hold any other office and that members of the House of Representatives, the "progressive" branch, be elected by districts for four year terms. He advocated that judges of the more important courts be appointed by the president with the advice and consent of the Senate and that the judges of the inferior courts be appointed by the governors with the advice and consent of the state senates. He believed that justices of the Supreme Court should be ineligible from holding any other governmental office. He also urged that government officials have fixed salaries not to be changed during their terms.

Burnett thought that his reforms, by making officials more independent and not allowing certain ones to hold any other offices (e.g., senators could not use their offices as a way to the presidency), would help "to secure the honesty of officers, by the simple and effectual method of removing the temptation to do wrong. Human virtue is always most secure in the absence of temptation."

This is not the place, perhaps, to explore the merits of Burnett's various proposals, but it is important to note, I think, that he could quite clearly distinguish between his patriotism to the nation and his evaluation (in some cases very negative) of the constitutional regime. This should be a more common characteristic amongst Americans, especially U.S. Catholics.

What do we see, then, when we look back on Peter Burnett? He was a principled man, a banker who was wary of wealth, a pioneer who did much, as both a practical politician and a propagandist-theoretician, to establish effective civil government in the Anglo-American tradition on the west coast. He took time to write two large books of apologetics. If his understanding of the role of government was perhaps too limited, he still brought to bear on governmental problems a combination of common sense and creativity. It would be too much to say that Catholic public officials and politicians should take him as a model. It would be too little to say that such men have nothing to learn from him and his life.

Bibliography

Burnett, Peter Hardeman. *The American Theory of Government with Reference to the Present Crisis* (New and Enlarged Edition). New York, 1863.

Burnett, Peter Hardeman. *The Path Which Led a Protestant Lawyer to the Catholic Church*. New York: D. Appleton, 1860.

Burnett, Peter Hardeman. *Reasons Why We Should Believe in God, Love God and Obey God*. New Ycrk: Catholic Publication Society, 1884.

Burnett, Peter Hardeman. *Recollections and Opinions of an Old Pioneer*. New York: D. Appleton & Company, 1880.

Caughey, John W. and Norris Hundley, Jr. *California: History of a Remarkable State* (Fourth Edition). Englewood Cliffs, N.J.: Prentice-Hall, Inc., c. 1982.

Hunt, Rockwell D. and Nellie Van De Grift Sanchez. *A Short History of California*. New York: Thomas Y. Crowell Company, c. 1929.

Johnson, Allen and Dumas Malone (editors). *Dictionary of American Biography*. New York: Charles Scribner's Sons, c. 1958-1964.

"Burnett, Peter Hardeman," Volume II, pages 300-301.

Lavender, David. *Land of Giants: The Drive to the Pacific Northwest, 1750-1950.* Lincoln, Neb.: University of Nebraska Press, 1979.

National Cyclopaedia of American Biography. New York: James T. White & Company, 1897. "Burnett, Peter Hardeman," Volume IV, pages 105-106.

9

James Campbell: Civic Leader, Judge, and Presidential Cabinet Member (1812-1893)

STEPHEN M. KRASON

I wish to acknowledge the assistance of Professor Jack R. Boyde of Franciscan University of Steubenville in doing the research for this essay.

During the first hundred years of the United States, only two Catholics served in the cabinets of presidents, Roger Brooke Taney and James Campbell. Campbell is much less well known than the Marylander that was born a generation before him and rose to the highest judicial office in the land, but he is, in many ways, as interesting of a subject of study for a book like this. This is for the following reasons: first, his legal and political career was about as multifaceted as Taney's — even though, while highly respected, he never attained the stature in the bar the latter did —; like Taney, he had important influence on national political developments during the part of his career when he was in active politics, although in a less obvious way; both were, mostly for different reasons, controversial figures in their time who faced much enmity from certain quarters; both seem to have been men who, in a quiet way, were devout in their Catholicism and this can be identified in their public lives; and, finally, unlike Taney, he confronted considerable overt, hostile religious bigotry throughout his career. Indeed, there seems to be little doubt that had it not been for this, he would have risen to much higher office, been a more significant figure on the national scene for a longer period of time, and gained much more fame. Indeed, he might well have attained the heights Taney did. It seems that the cross God gave James Campbell to bear was that his judicial and political career took place at a time when anti-Catholic Nativist sentiment — which I speak about below — was raging at a fever pitch. This clearly seems to have been the major factor which stymied the further development of his public career.

Early Life and Early Legal Career

James Campbell was born on September 1, 1812 in Southwark, Pennsylvania, now a part of Philadelphia. His parents were Anthony Campbell and Catherine McGarvey Campbell, both of Irish descent. They were members of old St. Mary's Parish, famed for having what was apparently the first parochial school in the country. His father, an immigrant, was involved in the conflicts surrounding the Hogan Schism, which Church historian Theodore Maynard calls "the gravest schism of the American Church." The Schism grew out of the controversy about "trusteeism," in which the demand was being made that lay trustees of parishes, instead of the bishop, be permitted to decide who their pastors should be, in the manner of many Protestant denominations. Although involving a question of lay preroga-tives, the controversy, like most schisms, was apparently instigated by clerics. In Philadelphia, the Schism essentially pitted followers of Father William Hogan against the bishop, and broke out into riots. Anthony Campbell, an opponent of the Hoganites, was seriously injured in one confrontation with them.

The best source of information we have about James Campbell's life, taking into account its expected complimentarity, is a biographical essay by his son John M. Campbell, Esq., in the *Records of the American Catholic Historical Society of Philadelphia* (1894). In it and other brief sketches of Campbell, such as the one in J. Herman Schauinger's *Profiles in Action* (which appears to have been composed with the essay as its primary source), there is no mention of his having siblings. Campbell's son describes his grandfather, Anthony Campbell, as "a highly esteemed merchant." He indicates that the reason James Campbell's parents sent him to a private school instead of a public one was either a concern about the quality of education at the latter or for social reasons, since "only the children of the very poor attended" public schools then. The school he was sent to was run by two old schoolmasters, Geraldus and John Stockdale, who were strict disciplinarians. They apparently had a very positive effect on James, who became very studious and even, in his later years in the school, was allowed to teach classes. He was so studious, in fact, that his mother often forced him to put aside his work to get more into play. He developed a lifelong affection for books, becoming a subscriber to the Philadelphia Library at twenty and often telling his children that, "A book is the best friend of man or woman; one need never feel lonely if once he acquire the habit of reading." The diary that he kept for a very brief period — twenty-four days, in 1836 — shows that reading played an important part of each routine day for him: newspapers, legal manuals and case reports, a Greek grammar, biography, periodicals, poetry, and other books.

Campbell read law in the office of Edward D. Ingraham, who his son describes as "one of the most prominent lawyers of his day," and was admitted to the bar at age twenty-one. His son writes that "he soon acquired a very lucrative [law] practice." He did not marry until 1845, at the age of thirty-three. His wife was Emilie S. Chapron, whose father was also an important merchant in Philadelphia. They had only two children: Anthony Chapron

Campbell and John M. Campbell. His wife lived only twelve years after they married. These years, however, were the main ones of his public career, so she was able to share that with him. His sons were still young at the time of her passing, but he raised them on his own and remained a widower the rest of his life. The obvious, considerable admiration expressed for him by his son in the biographical essay makes one think he was a very good father. His son does not speak specifically about his mother, so we cannot say much about Campbell's relationship with his wife. The general, very positive tone of the essay makes one think it was a very good marriage, however, which was lacking in serious conflicts or crises between the couple. The essay does indicate that Campbell was a faithful, dutiful husband when it says: "His private life was sincere and blameless, unstained with even a suspicion of immorality or impurity of any description."

Early Involvement in Politics

Campbell's son writes that "[h]e leaped at once into the political arena" after admission to the bar, and his diary entries demonstrate this and his associations with friends of similar interest. He also had become a member of the Philadelphia Athenaeum and the local debating society. He attained his first public position in 1840, when he was only in his twenty-seventh year. It was an appointive position, the equivalent of a member of the local school board today. He was appointed by the Commissioners of Southwark — the elected commissioners of his town were responsible for appointing school directors (i.e., school board members) — as a "Director of the Public Schools for the education of children at the public expense for the Third Section of the First School District of the State of Pennsylvania." The First District directors elected one from among themselves to represent them as Comptroller — representative from their District — on the Central Board, a board above the district board. It was a kind of two-level board of education system. In late 1840, the First District directors elected Campbell as their Comptroller. One wonders if his quick elevation by his peers was not due to this legal background — much as the substantial responsibilities given to the youthful Taney when first elected to the Maryland legislature were due to this — especially since school board members have not primarily been lawyers. Campbell also became a member of the High School Committee of the Board. There was only one public high school then in existence in the larger district, Boys' High School, which this Committee was responsible for overseeing.

It was the subject of high school education that Campbell was involved in what one might call his first public controversy. He offered a resolution in September 1841 to establish a public high school for girls for the purpose of training teachers. As his son writes, however, "the feeling against the higher education of women was so strong" that the proposal was defeated by the Central Board 10 to 9. A girls' high school of this sort would have to wait another eight years to be established, long after Campbell had left the Board.

Two thoughts come to mind here. One is that it is curious that Campbell's first office was on a public school board, when he got his schooling under private auspices after his parents spurned the public schools for him. Second, at the risk of making a tortured attempt to see relevance in the action, one wonders if his promoting secondary education for women could have had its basis, ultimately, in his Catholic, or at least Christian, beliefs. There is no way of knowing, of course. Perhaps it was an expression of a general sense of fairness that these beliefs gave him.

It was around this same time that Campbell first became involved in national politics. He became a partisan of President John Tyler. Tyler had one of the most interesting political careers of any American president. He had been a Jacksonian Democrat, but then broke with Jackson even while retaining much of his general political perspective. He was a man who readily followed his own political beliefs even when they set him against his party. Even while remaining a Democrat, he was elected vice president in 1840 running on a ticket which the Whig William Henry Harrison headed. Harrison, of course, died after only one month in office and Tyler became president. His independence asserted itself: he refused to let the Harrison Whig cabinet control his presidency (and, eventually, after he refused to go along with the Whig effort for a new national bank, it resigned). His relations with the Whig-dominated Congress thus became sour and government was deadlocked during his administration, with limited legislative accomplishment. The disaffected Democrat Tyler, at odds with the Whigs, apparently had hopes of establishing a third party, but didn't succeed. Campbell's son makes the following ambiguous statement about why his father was motivated to support Tyler:

> In those days, the politics of the city were controlled by a select few. Thomas D. Grover, William E. Alexander, John Oakford and others, were my father's associates. He was shrewd enough to see that if the President did not succeed in one way he would in another. If he could not build up a third party, at least he would disrupt one of the old — the Whig. It was, therefore, a good movement to foster his ambition, and with Tyson [one of his Philadelphia friends and political associates] and others, my father joined the Tyler interest. He soon became one of its moving spirits in Philadelphia, and, as it proved, to the advancement of his own fortunes.

Campbell, then, seems to have been attracted to Tyler for one or the other of these reasons, or a combination of them: support for Tyler's views, which, of course, could be expected to be carried over to a new party; simply a dislike of Whig ideas or thinking (indeed, many Philadelphia Whigs of the time were antagonistic to the Irish Catholics and the American Whig party generally tended to attract the Nativists); a perception that following Tyler could lead to an opportunity to oust the ruling political powers in Philadelphia; the fact that he was close to people who were pro-Tyler (his brief diary mentions Tyson quite a bit); or, purely and simply, he saw it as a way of furthering his political ambitions. We do not know for sure what the answer was, so it is difficult to come to any conclusion about what this decision tells us about Campbell. I am inclined against thinking the last possibility was, by itself or perhaps predominantly, the explanation. It suggests an opportunism which does not seem to have been in character for Campbell, as this essay should make apparent. Moreover, the local Whig hostility to the Irish, the closeness of many of the Philadelphia Irish to the Jacksonian Democrats (and thus their opposition to the Whigs), and Campbell's own Democratic party affiliation as his career progressed makes one think his embracing of Tyler was due mostly to his agreement with the President's philosophical-political orientation.

What came of Campbell's support of Tyler was that he gained sufficient access to the President to be able to play a role in helping him reshape his cabinet after the resignations. Tyler, seeking to gain political strength in Pennsylvania, appointed James Madison Porter, Esq. of Easton, Pennsylvania as his new Secretary of War. John Campbell says Porter's selection "was accomplished chiefly through the efforts of my father." Tyler, apparently, began to recognize Campbell as an important young political leader in the state. Campbell's rising reputation was also being noticed there. In 1842, Democratic Governor David Rittenhouse Porter — apparently not related to James Madison Porter, so it probably was not a return political favor to Campbell — appointed him to the Court of Common Pleas for the City and County of Philadelphia when he was just twenty-nine. He was to serve in that capacity for the next ten years.

Judgeship, State Attorney Generalship, and Target of Nativists

It was at this point that Campbell began to be the focus of anti-Catholic attacks. The 1840s, a time of substantially increased immigration (not all of it Catholic), saw a sharp rise of Nativist sentiment. There was some objection to Campbell's appointment to the bench. As his son writes, "it was counted a grievance that the son of an Irish Catholic should be raised to so high an office so early in life." The opposition did not become too intense, however, because his background and character were sterling, and, to quote John Campbell, "he was known to be clear headed, intelligent, upright and studious, and quick to grasp at any legal point." It was in this same year of 1842 that a development occurred which would lead, in 1844, to what Maynard calls "the fiercest explosion" of Nativism and thrust Campbell into the center of the conflict. Bishop Francis Patrick Kenrick of Philadelphia petitioned the public school board in November 1842 to substitute the use of the Douay version of the Bible for the Protestant version for the use of the Catholic children in the city's public schools (Pennsylvania had a practice of reading Bible verses at the start of the school day up to 1963, when the Supreme Court declared it unconstitutional). Kenrick had state law on his side — it said that "the religious predilections of the parents shall be respected" — and he was not asking for total elimination of Bible reading in the schools. Nevertheless, his action was a provocation to the Nativists whose leaders were only too ready to twist it to suit their purposes. The ultimate result was the Kensington riots of May 1844, which cost thirteen lives, many injuries, and the destruction by fire of two Catholic churches and damage to other Catholic Church buildings. The Nativist mob headed for Campbell's house; as his son put it, he had "thrown himself heart and soul into the struggle, organized the Irish Catholic interest, and became its head and front." As the mob was about to torch his house, one of their leaders, an Andrew McClain, who had been a boyhood friend of Campbell's and whose parents in spite of religious differences had been close to the latter's, rushed to the front and stopped them. As John Campbell writes, McClain "was a man of great size and strength, and of that commanding presence which can hold in check even a mob at a crisis." Campbell's house and possibly also his life were saved because of this act.

The next time Judge Campbell was to become the target of the Nativists — possibly because they remembered his leadership of the Irish Catholics at the time of the riots — was when he ran for a seat on the Pennsylvania Supreme Court in 1851. The year before — riding the crest of the Jacksonian spirit which held that as many public offices as possible should be elective — Pennsylvanians had amended their constitution to provide for an elective judiciary. The Democrats were strong in Pennsylvania and all the four other candidates on their slate for the Court except for Campbell were elected. He lost by about 3200 votes statewide out of over 355,000 cast. The accounts of Campbell's life leave no doubt that he lost purely because of anti-Catholicism. His son writes — probably because they were so many Democratic party adherents in the state and all the other Democrats won — that it illustrated that even while the Democrats purported to have "great contempt" for Nativist sentiment, "there was not a little of the spirit among themselves."

Actually, though, as often happens in life, this defeat was a sort of blessing in disguise for Campbell, ultimately being responsible for propelling him into a national office. There was an election for governor of Pennsylvania in the fall of 1851. The Democrats were worried about winning because they needed the Irish Catholic vote, centered mostly in Philadelphia, and were afraid that as a backlash against what had just happened to Campbell it might not come their way. Indeed, the Irish were very discontented and bitter, seeing Campbell's defeat, as his son put it, "as a direct blow at their religious faith." The Democratic gubernatorial candidate was William Bigler of Clearfield County who was part of the James Buchanan faction of the party. Apparently, Buchanan had helped secure his nomination as a means of laying the groundwork for his own bid for the presidency. Obviously, if Bigler lost it would be a serious setback for Buchanan, so the situation was of great concern to him. The Buchanan faction sought to enlist Campbell's support, knowing that, as both John Campbell and Schauinger write, only Judge Campbell could "control" the crucial Irish Catholic vote (this gives us a sense of exactly how politically prominent and powerful Campbell had become). John Campbell says that his father was already inclined to Bigler, so he quickly agreed to help. Moreover, he says that Campbell saw "in the not distant future the opportunity to pay his persecutors back in their own coin." By this, he seems to suggest not only that his father believed that Bigler's election, brought about by Irish support, would serve to rebuke the Nativists and show the Democrats among them just how vital this bloc was for the party, but also that it might result in his gaining some higher office in direct defiance of what they wanted and so soon after they had denied him. In effect, it would be an embarrassing slap in the face at them, but one they royally deserved. Can we fault Campbell for thinking this way? Was it vengeful? I think not. It was simply making a point that needed to be made and teaching Nativists a lesson about politics. It was something like the person who is belittled and told he can't succeed at something and then comes back, summons up his greatest determination, and puts forth his strongest effort to show that he can. Moreover, what was said above indicates that Campbell's decision to support Bigler was not unprincipled or cynically opportunistic: he favored him already, but supporting him promised additional advantages.

Campbell's expectations were indeed fulfilled. Bigler was elected and his first appointment was that of Campbell as State Attorney General (the Pennsylvania attorney generalship was at the time an appointive position). He was to serve only a little more than a year in this position before being elevated to the presidential cabinet, but during this time he presided over two very important cases which the Commonwealth of Pennsylvania was involved in. One was the *Wheeling Bridge Case*, mentioned in the Taney essay in this volume, in which Pennsylvania sought to have Virginia remove a bridge it had built over the Ohio River. The other was the *Parker Fugitive Slave Law Case*, which perhaps gives us a small insight into the influence of Campbell's religion or at least his moral sense on his public actions. As Attorney General he recognized that he had a duty to see to it that the Fugitive Slave Law — which made it incumbent on free states to return escaped slaves to their owners in the southern or border states and was then growing considerably in unpopularity in the North — was enforced. His son's essay makes it apparent that his father saw it this way. It might be difficult for some to understand how one could see it as his duty to do anything that would aid the sustenance of the evil of slavery. I, of course, have previously addressed this in the Taney essay in this volume. I will say here that if one has read St. Augustine and the speeches of Abraham Lincoln he will probably understand this better. Political life involves what a contemporary scholar of Lincoln, Professor Harry V. Jaffa, has called the "tension between principle and expediency" and it requires a heavy dose of the virtue of prudence. One must always keep moral principles in sight and never permit the adoption of a policy or course of action which will actually surrender or compromise the principle, treating it as if it no longer exists (actually, though, as I said in the Taney essay, the Church had not up to this time clearly taught that slavery was intrinsically evil). At the same time, he will often have to accept a very imperfect or partial realization or actualization of the principle in practice, in the course of day to day political life or public polity. To try to push for its full realization, he knows, will sometimes have the effect of creating a worse situation, which can result in a more full fledged attack on the principle itself or create other evils. This happens, of course, because of human attitudes, the prejudices and emotional fervor of people, and likely human reactions. The good and successful statesman — as opposed to merely *politician* — is one who understands this and has developed a sense of prudence, which is necessary to deal with and peaceably solve such dilemmas. Thus, carrying out one's duty even when involving something morally objectionable — so long as he knows and adheres to the moral principle in question — may in some circumstances be necessary and desirable to keep political life on an even keel and avert greater evils. St. Augustine, in fact, said that the Christian could even participate in certain immoral acts if his duties required it (the example he gave was the judge who had to sanction the use of torture to get at the truth, which was a common practice in the Roman Empire of his time). It was better that Christians follow this course than eschew political life entirely, which would prevent their witness from being brought to it and eventually eliminating such practices.

The *Parker* case involved a black girl who had been forcibly removed from Chester County, Pennsylvania and taken to Baltimore, Maryland (Maryland was a slave state) by people who claimed that they had title to her because she had been born in slavery.   Campbell, with the considerable assistance of a Protestant minister from Chester County named Rev. John M. Dickie, was able to establish that the girl had actually been born free. He argued the case in a Maryland court against two leading members of the Maryland bar. The court agreed with him and the girl was permitted to go free. In a small way, this case tells some things about Campbell's character. First, it is apparent that even though he argued the case for the girl's freedom he would have been prepared, had the evidence indicated otherwise, to follow the Fugitive Slave Law and not pursue the case. This suggests courage because, as stated, the Law was becoming more unpopular in his state and the North generally. As it was, he *did* pursue it because he became convinced of the girl's free birth, even though he had no obligation to do so and could just as easily have let it pass. It meant, as noted, that he had to take on two top Maryland lawyers on their home territory where his cause could not have been expected to have been popular. This further shows courage along with a certain self-confidence and also illustrates his integrity and his commitment to pursuing the truth. The depth of his commitment to truth and his willingness to listen to people are also demonstrated in the open reception he gave to Rev. Dickie when he brought forth the information about the girl to him. Moreover, it also tells us about how much he had developed professionally and personally when we consider that his diary indicates that earlier in his career he became extremely nervous when he went into the courtroom, suggesting a certain lack of confidence. Years later, in a letter about Rev. Dickie to the latter's son — written after Dickie's death — Campbell demonstrated another of the many highly commendable qualities of his character: his gratitude. He expressed how grateful he was to Dickie for taking such a substantial interest in the case and preparing so much of the material for him. Campbell said that "from that time I revered him ... and held his memory in the deepest respect."

It almost goes without saying that all of these qualities were shaped by his religious and moral training and probably reflect his religious commitment.

Post Master General of the United States

The 1852 presidential campaign and election took place while Campbell was Attorney General. Although Campbell did not have a national following he was a man of considerable political power in Pennsylvania, as I have said. However, since Pennsylvania had considerable national electoral importance at that time — Campbell's son writes that it "was the pivot upon which revolved all the fortunes of politics" — anybody who was a political power in the state had to be reckoned with nationally. This became apparent at the 1852 Democratic Convention and in the fall election. Campbell went to the Baltimore convention as a Buchanan supporter. Buchanan, who John Campbell portrays as unprincipled, treacherous, and ungrateful to his father in the years that followed (and it seems that Campbell himself didn't really trust the Buchanan faction) almost won the nomination, but was undone by his fellow Pennsylvanian Simon Cameron's maneuvering against him at the convention. The nomination fight was intense between four different candidates: Buchanan, Stephen Douglas, Lewis Cass, and William L. Marcy and went to the forty-ninth ballot, when Franklin Pierce of New Hampshire emerged as a kind of compromise candidate and won the nomination. Campbell stayed with Buchanan — delegates were in no way bound to candidates — until his defeat was certain. In the campaign that followed, Campbell put all his efforts into Pierce's election who he readily rallied around — his earlier support for Buchanan was understandable since he was a member of the pro-Buchanan Porter Administration — since Pierce had been a Tyler supporter. Actually, though, John Campbell indicates his father's attachment to the Democratic party was such a strong one that he was likely to support and try to deliver the vote of his Irish Catholic followers to virtually whomever the convention nominated. Pennsylvania was a crucial state for Pierce and Schauinger tells us that his carrying it "was largely due to Campbell and the Irish Catholics."

After the election, the latter fact motivated William L. Kirst, a leading Philadelphia lawyer and long-time friend of Campbell's who headed the Pennsylvania Democratic State Central Committee, to urge Pierce to reward Campbell's efforts by giving him an important post. When word got out that Pierce was considering this, the Nativist elements of the party objected. He brushed these objections aside, however, and appointed Campbell Post Master General; later he was, commendably, to defend his Administration and Campbell from Nativist attacks. One of Campbell's most bitter anti-Catholic assailants was a defrocked Catholic priest named Alessandro Gavazzi, an Italian native, who went around the U.S. publicly haranguing anything Catholic.

The above account of how Campbell got his cabinet post is from his son and Schauinger. Pierce biographer Roy Franklin Nichols and Buchanan biographer Philip Shriver Klein present a very different story. Nichols writes that Pierce made the decision at Buchanan's urging. Pierce had decided against appointing Buchanan or any other presidential aspirants, but was open to receiving Buchanan's advice about other appointees. Buchanan, Nichols and Klein say, suggested either Campbell or Governor Porter (Buchanan's letters confirm this.) Nichols also indicates that the cabinet was chosen with the intention of conciliating and representing all factions of the party, a practice which continued throughout Pierce's Administration and which some believe helped lead to its political failure. He says that Campbell and also Robert McClelland of Michigan (who he appointed Secretary of the Interior) were the choices of Buchanan and Cass. He even states that "Buchanan's faction . . . press[ed for] Campbell," but other elements from Pennsylvania seemed *less* interested in him. In the end, of course, Campbell *was* appointed and Pierce seemingly went back on his intention not to appoint a presidential aspirant when he named Marcy (from New York) as Secretary of State. It is possible, of course, that *both* sets of events occurred as part of the prelude to Campbell's appointment and both Kirst and Buchanan influenced Pierce's decision.

As it turned out, the cabinet was perhaps the most remarkable part of the Pierce Administration, which historians have often criticized for being lackluster, legislatively ineffective, and politically unsuccessful. Joining the above men were James Guthrie of Kentucky as Secretary of the Treasury, Jefferson Davis of Mississippi — later to become president of the Confederacy — as Secretary of War, Caleb Cushing of Massachusetts as Attorney General, and James C. Dobbin of North Carolina as Secretary of the Navy. It was a cabinet not only made up of representatives of different factions of the party, but pretty well mixed sectionally. Pierce made sure that they all agreed with his basic principles. It turned out to be a very stable cabinet; all of its members stayed in their offices until the end of the one-term administration. The Pierce Administration was also one which was untouched by scandal, kept the government out of debt (an accomplishment of which not all administrations even in the nineteenth century could boast), and seemed, within the cabinet (which comprised most of the executive branch in those days), to operate quite efficiently. For an administration considered a failure, it thus seems like it would have ranked quite favorably alongside most twentieth century ones. Moreover, the cabinet members seemed to get along very well and respect each other and the Administration was notably free of internal discord. If there was a disagreement about something, Pierce backed the man in whose department the matter lay. John Campbell (whose assessment is admittedly more glowing than the other sources consulted, although the others agree about the above points) claims these men "were the peers of any statesman of any time. They were men of thought and action — a rare combination. They were men of great mental abilities, of great knowledge, yet prompt and intrepid executive officers."

What can we say about Campbell's achievements as Post Master General and his role in the Administration in general? It appears that Pierce sought to involve his cabinet intimately in his decisionmaking. John Campbell writes that the cabinet members were Pierce's "confidential advisers, and not mere upper clerks as had been the case in certain other administrations." He gave them wide latitude; *they* were in charge of their departments. His policy was not to interfere unless it was clearly necessary. He essentially deferred to the cabinet members in making patronage appointments in their departments. He tried even to avoid letting other cabinet members intrude upon an individual member's appointments in his department even when they concerned the former's home state. For example, when Davis objected to some of Campbell's Mississippi appointments, Pierce upheld Campbell, but brought Davis around to the point of agreeing. When Campbell selected New York appointees and showed his list to Pierce, the latter suggested that, while it was acceptable to him, Campbell consult New Yorker Marcy. Marcy suggested a few changes which Campbell made. That, then, was the Pierce pattern: encourage consultation among the cabinet members where appropriate, allow the member making the appointment to virtually always make the final decision, but try to create support among all involved for the decision made.

It is a tribute to the integrity, dependability, trustworthiness, gentlemanliness, and willingness to get along and work as a team of Campbell and the others that the Pierce cabinet functioned as smoothly and harmoniously as it did.

Nichols' biography of Pierce gives a good summary of the highlights of Campbell's cabinet career. It is worth examining them year by year here, including his relations with an often uncooperative Congress which caused him much frustration. Even at this early time in American history, the postal bureaucracy was large. There were twenty-three thousand postmasters around the country. Most of these appointments came from Congressional recommendations and Campbell delegated most of these actual appointments to a subordinate. One of the main problems he faced when he took over the Department was its deficit, which he tried devotedly to end, but was frustrated continually in doing so, mostly because of Congressional action. Other major problems were inadequate international postal conventions with countries such as England, France, and Mexico and the difficulty of dealing with railroad and steamship companies who were charging the government extremely high rates to carry the mail and had become almost dependent on the revenues from it.

The above problems dominated Campbell's first report to Congress in 1853. He did not make many recommendations in it. He did recommend, in spite of the deficit, higher pay for postmasters and the hiring of some new personnel that he thought were needed.

In his report and recommendations to Congress in 1854, Campbell urged a system of registering valuable mail, which was adopted. He also called for increases in postage for newspapers, which brought the wrath of many editorial writers upon him and probably hurt the Pierce Administration's popularity. Congress also gave him money to enlarge the building housing the Post Office Department in Washington — it refused his request to build an entirely new building, in spite of the need — and, on its own, authorized the construction of a cross country telegraph line.

In 1856, his last full year, Campbell reported a set of disappointing results to Congress. He could not claim progress on solving the major problems that had faced him from the start. He had cut the deficit at first, but then the postmaster pay hike — much higher as passed by Congress than he had recommended — and Congress's imposition of a costly Mississippi River mail service — which he had opposed — caused it to climb to the highest levels in the Department's history.

Schauinger says that at the end of the Pierce Administration, Campbell "perhaps felt the most dissatisfied of the cabinet members," basically because of the above failures and developments. Nevertheless, he did have various specific achievements. Besides the registered mail system and the expansion of domestic service, he improved contract practices, established the requirement that all mail be prepaid instead of paid for by the recipient (which contributed considerably to efficiency), introduced stamped envelopes and improved postage stamps so the user no longer had to cut them off of large sheets (which was the only way they could previously be bought), expanded overseas service and, despite failing in most of his efforts to get more favorable rates from foreign countries, did succeed with Germany. He also sought to root out irregularities in the Chicago post office by removing the local postmaster, but

Douglas, the Senator from Illinois, blocked him. He was not alone among the members of the Pierce Cabinet in having Congress stymie him from further success.

Perhaps another reason for his disappointment was Campbell's political failure. In spite of his cabinet duties, he was able to keep a finger in Pennsylvania politics. His faction, with his leadership, attempted in 1855 to round up support in the Democratic party there for Pierce's renomination and gain control of the state party organization. They were beaten by the Buchanan forces and, of course, in 1856 the latter took advantage of Pierce's weakness and unpopularity and secured the nomination, and the presidency, for himself.

Campbell appears to have had some influence with Pierce in other areas of Administration policymaking outside of the realm of his Department. In his discussion of the Pierce cabinet, however, Davis' biographer William E. Dodd does not list him among its more "forceful members" (which may mean he was not among its more influential ones). Nichols, however, suggests that his and Cushing's purported anti-British attitudes may have helped influence the suspicion the Administration exhibited toward Great Britain in its foreign policy. Pierce apparently consulted his cabinet on the Kansas-Nebraska Bill and then they all pushed hard for it. The Bill, whose biggest Congressional proponent was Senator Douglas, repealed the Missouri Compromise of 1820 limiting slavery to the area south of 36°30' and instead established the principle of "squatter sovereignty" whereby the settlers of the new Western territories would vote on whether or not to have slavery. While it was seen as a compromise, it actually had the effect of precipitating a civil war in Kansas as settlers from both North and South poured into the Territory in the hope of swaying the slavery decision one way or the other. Campbell seems to have favored "squatter sovereignty" in principle — not just to meet the exigency of the situation — indicating agreement with the Southern thinking that, as he put it, "the people alone [should] ... say what institutions they will have amongst them." He also was responsible for Pierce's appointment of Andrew H. Reeder of Easton, Pennsylvania as Kansas' first territorial governor.

Campbell's endorsement of the Kansas-Nebraska Bill and "squatter sovereignty" deserves a comment. I mentioned the need of the man in politics to maintain the "Lincolnian tension between principle and expediency." It was on this very question of "squatter sovereignty" that Professor Jaffa states that Lincoln so clearly exemplified the ability to do this. Endorsing "squatter sovereignty" undermined this tension, this need to keep principle and expediency in balance, because it had the effect of discarding a basic principle of our Declaration of Independence — and of our political order — that all men are created equal, by the fact that it permitted some men to decide whether the equality of other men would be respected or not by voting whether or not they should be enslaved. True, our political order for some time would have to tolerate, in actual practice, a critical deviation from our Founding principles — the institution of slavery — for the sake of political reality, indeed, for the sake of its continued unity and civil peace. (Thus greater or compounded evils would develop if there were an uncompromising attempt to put the principle into practice quickly.) "Squatter sovereignty," however, was not just tolerating slavery; it also provided a justification for it in principle. It represented an obliviousness to the fundamental principle mentioned above and thus signalled its surrender. It was not just a compromise in praxis but also, and most essentially, in principle. It treated the principle of "all men are created equal" as if it no longer existed.

If Campbell seemed to understand the problem of the statesman's role in maintaining the "tension between principle and expediency" in the *Parker Fugitive Slave Case*, he obviously did not on the Kansas-Nebraska Bill. Not only did he not see the constitutional and philosophical danger it posed, but he, as a Christian, did not see the moral and religious problems it presented. First, it amounted to an official moral acceptance of slavery — an official indifference to it can be judged to show an acceptance — so long as the people wanted it, even though our constitutional tradition and the principles underlying it could not sanction such an acceptance. Second, more disturbingly, we see in Campbell's words above a seeming willingness to assert that a (presumed) principle of democracy — that a practice should be allowed to prevail so long as it's voted for — should be allowed to take precedence over all other considerations even when the matter being dealt with is one of morality, and, in fact, is conceded to be immoral. The latter seems to be like the attitude of so many of our present-day politicians, Catholic and otherwise, on abortion. Thus, Campbell's view on the Bill betrayed both a confusion about the true nature of our constitutional principles and which should take precedence — i.e., majority rule, as vital as it is, was never held by our Founding Fathers to be able to supersede natural rights of individuals — and about which side one should come down on when there is a conflict between a political-constitutional principle and a moral-religious one (presuming that the former was correct in the first place, which it wasn't here).

There is not much, in my judgment, which can excuse Campbell's confusion about what the correct priority of political-constitutional principles was in this case, unless it is simply the fact that he was too much a man of action and not enough of a political thinker. On the other conflict, we cannot say a sense of duty would have excused his support for the Kansas-Nebraska Bill, as with enforcing the Fugitive Slave Law. He had no duty to commend it or even support it, as he seems to have done, within the councils of the Pierce Administration — even if we could understand a willingness to stand by and even officially defend the decision once the Administration adopted it. An important consideration, however, as with Taney in the *Dred Scott* case, is the Church's then uncertain teaching about the intrinsic immorality of slavery. We may actually be too harsh in judging, then, that he allowed a political-constitutional principle (majority rule) to take precedence over a clear moral-religious one. It, then, perhaps could not really have been judged — in its time — in the same light as abortion and our politicians today. Still, it was clear that slavery was a moral issue, and that it did not involve an easily justifiable relationship of one person over another (i.e., a master owning and totally controlling a slave), and so Campbell might still be faulted for thinking that majority rule should take precedence over any consideration of this in public policy.

We shall not belabor the point. As far as Campbell's overall cabinet performance is concerned, we can say that he was hard-working, businesslike, apparently well-regarded by Pierce, and that his Department was run efficiently and honestly. He was not the penny-pinch some in Congress accused him of being; rather, like any good businessman, he tried hard to economize but would spend money when there was a demonstrated need. Even if he thought when he left he had failed in many ways, he must be judged to have made some valuable long-run contributions to the Post Office Department.

Still, he probably contributed to the unpopularity of the Pierce Administration. Even though its lack of legislative accomplishment — seemingly more due to Congress's obstructionism than anything else — its even handed approach to all factions of the Democratic party which resulted in none being too well rewarded or too enthusiastic about it, and the heightening sectional conflict within the party over slavery, were probably the primary reasons for this (and precluded Pierce's renomination). Campbell's tough decisions on economy in his Department, noted above, and his Catholicism in a decade when Nativism reached its zenith didn't help. Although, as mentioned, his Catholicism caused some initial objections to Pierce appointing him, it did not deter his doing so and Campbell and the rest of the cabinet were approved quickly by the Senate. Once in office Pierce supported Campbell strongly against anti-Catholic attacks and tolerated no Know-Nothing sympathies (as this most virulent form of Nativism which emerged in the 1850s was called). He even removed Know-Nothing supporters from federal offices in the face of charges that the Catholic Church was controlling him. He and Campbell brushed off such completely false charges as the claim that the hierarchy had arranged Campbell's appointment and — made by the *Cincinnati Gazette* newspaper — that Campbell had ousted many Protestant postal employees and replaced them with Catholics. Overall, though, it was perhaps true that, as Nichols states, Pierce's choice of Campbell "was a monument of enlightened tolerance but not of political foresight" and, as A. K. McClure writes in his *Old Time Notes of Pennsylvania*, it "aided very materially in the second Native American eruption... Know Nothingism in 1854." If Pierce lost popularity because of Campbell, he did win, as Nichols writes, the latter's "intense gratitude," and Campbell's son makes clear how deep and abiding it was. The two men were close friends the rest of their lives.

After Pierce's renomination was clearly out of the question, Campbell supported his fellow Pennsylvanian Buchanan, and apparently did so wholeheartedly. In fact, as John Campbell says, "[T]he whole power" of Pierce's Administration "was brought to bear upon his support." Campbell worked hard and successfully to line up the Philadelphia Irish Catholic support for Buchanan, which helped him carry Pennsylvania. The latter, along with the South that so favored him, won the election for him. An interesting occurrence took place before the Democratic Convention, when William Cassidy, editor of the *Albany Argus* newspaper, tried to promote Campbell for vice president. Although impractical since both he and Buchanan were from the same state and the restive South wanted one of its own on the ticket, he could have used the idea to help control the Pennsylvania delegation for other purposes. He spurned this idea, however; his son says the reason was because it would have hurt Buchanan's and the party's chances in November.

Later Political Efforts

Buchanan's victory meant that Campbell was returned to private life — permanently, as it turned out — at the age of forty-five. It was later in the year of his retirement, 1857, that Campbell's wife died. He had been one of the youngest men ever appointed to a presidential cabinet up to that time. He apparently was not considered by Buchanan for any post. He was never part of Buchanan's faction, in spite of his 1852 support for him; Schauinger simply says that they "regarded him" with "coolness." John Campbell bluntly states that, for all his efforts for Buchanan, his father "was rewarded with the blackest ingratitude." He also says — as noted, this does not concur with Nichols' and Klein's discussion of the circumstances surrounding Campbell's appointment — that Buchanan was particularly miffed that a man who Pierce had appointed from Buchanan's own state "in despite of his silent protest" had actually been proposed as his vice presidential running mate. After this, Campbell seems to have been treated rudely by the Buchanan people and, in fact, his son says that they put the word out that no friend of Campbell's could expect a favor from Buchanan.

Campbell very nearly returned to public life in 1861 when he sought one of Pennsylvania's U.S. Senate seats. In those days, state legislatures, not the voters, directly elected senators. In 1861, the Democrats had control of the state legislature, so the election of someone from that party was very likely. Campbell lost the Democratic nomination for the seat in the party's caucus — gaining the nomination would have been tantamount to election — by only a couple of votes. Again, Campbell's career was stymied by wrongful action. His defeat occurred because of the bribery of one of his supporters.

Campbell was minimally, but significantly, involved in the 1860 presidential election. In the summer of that year, his old cabinet colleague Jefferson Davis visited him and told him of the widespread animosity and successionist feeling in the South and the certainty of its intensification in the event of the election of Lincoln, which seemed very likely. He thought that the Democrats could carry Pennsylvania and thus perhaps head off Lincoln with a compromise electoral ticket of Douglas and John C. Breckinridge. Campbell jolted him by telling him of his certainty that Lincoln would win the state and the election. He suggested that they let Lincoln serve his term and — indicating that he would then put everything he had into a Democratic campaign after that and that he was apparently confident that he could effect the outcome in crucial Pennsylvania — said, "I pledge my life that his successor will be a Democrat!" After that day, the two men never again met. Campbell tried that fall to get Douglas and Breckenridge to withdraw to be replaced by Pierce as a last hope of defeating Lincoln but Pierce refused. (Davis and others apparently also favored this course of action, but there is no evidence that he was in league with his former cabinet colleague in approaching Pierce.) Pierce agreed that they should step aside, along with John Bell of the Constitutional Union party which also feared Lincoln's election would fracture the Union, but said the alternative ticket should be comprised of his former Treasury Secretary Guthrie and Horatio Seymour. Nichols claims that Davis and Campbell both jumped on this idea and tried to promote it — again, however, Campbell's son's remarks indicate it was unlikely they worked concertedly — but to no avail. We can see, then, that Campbell made a genuine effort, to the extent that he was in the position to do so, to save both his party and the Union in 1860.

Civic Leader

After the beginning of the 1860s Campbell, now ensconced in private life, turned his efforts to law practice and civic and charitable activities. As long ago as 1848, he had been appointed to the Board of Directors of St. Joseph's Orphan Asylum, the first Catholic orphanage in the U.S. He remained on that Board until his death, forty-five years later. It was probably the charity to which he was closest and devoted most of his efforts to. He was largely responsible for its financial affairs for many years and showed his considerable business acumen in this task. As Schauinger says, "its finances prospered under his care," and under his management it was able to expand considerably. As Bishop William O'Hara said at Campbell's funeral Mass, "his interest in the little orphans" there "was never relaxed" after his initial involvement.

He was also one of the original members of the Board of Directors of Girard College, a charitable institution set up by famous Philadelphia business leader Stephen Girard for the education of orphan boys. He served in that capacity for twenty-one years until his death. As with St. Joseph's, Campbell's was not merely the passive, almost honorific, role we often associate with members of the boards of such organizations today. He was active on Board committees. As his son and Schauinger tell us, he made weekly visits to the College and spent every Thursday in the classrooms. He was particularly involved in the religious training of the Catholic boys there. He knew the names of all the boys in the senior class and tried to find jobs for them when they graduated which would suit their individual talents and abilities. As his son put it, "[h]e . . . considered the helpless orphans . . . committed to his care as much entitled to his protection as were his own children." He was instrumental, as at St. Joseph's, in the expansion of the College's programs. At his death, the Board adopted a glowing resolution of commendation and gratitude, saying his many efforts "won the esteem and friendship of his associates." He received a similar commendation from the alumni association of the College.

For twenty-five years, he also served as a trustee of Jefferson Medical College and was its president two years. Again, this activity received his care and attention. Every Sunday he visited the patients in the College's hospital and inquired personally about their needs and wants, and about whether they found their care wanting in any way.

In 1869, Campbell was appointed a Director on the Board of City Trusts by the judges of the state Supreme Court and the Philadelphia Common Pleas Court. It oversaw many of Philadelphia's charitable institutions, including Girard College. Schauinger refers to it as "the Community Chest of its day." He also remained in this capacity until his death.

Campbell thus distinguished himself in the last thirty or so years of his life as an important civic leader in Philadelphia.

He died on January 27, 1893 in his eighty-first year. He had been healthy and active until only shortly before.

Campbell's Character and Religious Commitment

The above are the important events and activities of Campbell's life. I have already said some things about his character and religious commitment, but I consider this further now. His various endeavors, as noted, make clear his honesty, integrity, industriousness, and general good morals and there was little disagreement about this. Some even called him "strait-laced." He apparently was a humble man, in attitude as well as demeanor. He even asked that no sermon be preached at his funeral Mass. He was firm and determined — his son says "courageous," and we have given evidence of this — and from all indications decisive. Somewhat along these lines, his diary suggests that he stressed self-improvement. He also obviously committed himself fully to his undertakings. His gratitude for people's efforts on his behalf and his respect and good rapport with others have been commented on, and his devotedness to his friends — emphasized by his son — perhaps is also apparent from what has been said. Similarly, there is no question about his charity, not just in a general humanitarian sense but to people as individuals whom he was responsible for. He seems to have been trustworthy. His feathers were not easily ruffled; he appears to have been a man not easily driven to anger. An insight into the depths of some of these qualities and the presence of one other highly commendable one was given by Bishop O'Hara at his funeral. Campbell, he said, "car[ed] nothing for the dross of the world, but walk[ed] in the path that made him most acceptable to God." In his public career, "he endeavored to discharge his duties with fidelity to his conscience." As a judge, specifically, "he tempered justice with mercy."

On the negative side perhaps — although no doubt at times it was actually a desirable quality to have — we might note that he had a tendency to stubbornness. Perhaps this was because of his insistent determination and firmness.

In demeanor, Campbell was a quiet man, but not without a lightness and sense of humor. He was intelligent, methodical, and not known for great eloquence. He seems to have carried his points by the force of his reasoning, not a brilliance of presentation. He seems to have been an eminently practical and prudent man, and made clear that he had little regard for men whose "visionary schemes" caused them to ignore what was happening around them, especially in politics.

What, then, can we say about Campbell's religious commitment and spiritual life? Some points uncovered make one wonder how deeply religious he was. For example, *The Dictionary of American Biography*, in a terse article, says without elaboration that he was "loyal" to his Church "[t]hough not a strict religionist." It is unclear, of course, what this means. We notice from his diary (written before his public career started) that, early in his life, he apparently did not attend daily Mass, a practice generally associated with the pious Catholic who is able to do so, even though he had ready access to a church. It also leaves uncertain whether he attended Mass every Sunday (he records this for some Sundays, but not others). The other, and more substantial, evidence however, indicates that he was serious about and motivated by his Faith, but not ostentatious about it. For example, we know he was a member of St. Mary's Parish. He defended his Church and its people during the Nativist controversies, at considerable risk and costs to himself. His son emphasizes this, but so do other sources. He stayed firm in his Faith in the face of the Nativist onslaught and seems never to have even thought of renouncing Catholicism to advance — indeed, to make possible, for the most part — his political career. He demonstrates in his diary a sense of gratitude to God for his blessings as he seems to be discovering, as a young man, the unfortunate lot that certain people find themselves in (this perhaps led him into his charitable work). His extensive Catholic and other charitable work speaks for itself. Also, the comments of Bishop O'Hara at his funeral indicate both that he practiced his faith — regardless of whether he did so regularly as a *young* man or not — and believed in the power of prayer. Something his son says about the years of his life after his public career suggests he visited church often. O'Hara also characterizes him as apparently a fervent Catholic — "a man of strong faith" which was exhibited in his actions, especially in his political career and charitable work. He said that the faith his parents instilled in him "made an impression upon his heart which was never removed during his whole life." Indeed, the fact that many priests attended his funeral Mass seems to further confirm his active Catholicism. Finally, the manner of his death, as recorded by his son, suggests much faith. He says that Campbell "retained his faculties until the last moment, and contemplated the change that must come to all, without fear and with sublime Catholic resignation."

We are led to the conclusion that the way Campbell conducted his public career, his sacrifices, his courage and readiness in defending his Church when under attack, his good morals and apparent religious commitment made him — in spite of the concerns raised in connection with his support of the Kansas-Nebraska Bill — well-nigh an exemplary Catholic statesman. It is unfortunate that he was not able to have a longer public career.

Bibliography

Campbell, John M. "Biographical Sketch of Hon. James Campbell." *Records of the American Catholic Historical Society of Philadelphia*. Vol. V, No. 3 (1894).

Dodd, William E. *Jefferson Davis*. New York: Russell and Russell, 1966. (Originally published in 1907.) (Brief mention of Campbell.)

Klein, Philip Shriver. *President James Buchanan: A Biography*. University Park, Pa.: Penn State Univ. Press, 1962 (brief mention of Campbell).

Nichols, Roy Franklin. *Franklin Pierce: Young Hickory of the Granite Hills*. Philadelphia: U. of Pennsylvania Press, 1931.

Schauinger, J. Herman. *Profiles in Action: American Catholics in Public Life*. Milwaukee: Bruce, 1966.

Index

A

Ableman v. Booth, 151-152, 159
abolitionism and abolitionists
  (see also slaves and slavery),
  151, 154, 159, 175
abortion, 220
Acre, 80
Acton, Lord, 59
Adam (first parent), 10, 168
Adams, John Quincy, 106
Adams, John, 15, 37, 53, 54, 64,
  77, 129
Adams, Samuel, 52, 53, 54
African Episcopal Church of St.
  Thomas (first black church in
  U.S.) (see blacks [Negroes])
Albany Argus (newspaper), 221
alcohol (liquor), 91, 148
Alcott, Bronson, 169, 185
Alexander, William E., 204
Alexandria, Va.,90
America *(see* United States of
  America)
American Colonization Society,
  157
*American Insurance Co. v.
  Canter,* 156
American Republic, The (book),
  168, 176, 180, 183
American Revolution
  (Revolutionary War) *(see*
  United States of America)
*American Theory of Government
  Considered with Reference to
  the Present Crisis* (book), 195
Ames, Fisher, 75
Anderson, Roger Brooke Taney,
  141
angels, 57
Anglicanism *(see also*
  Protestantism; religion), 19, 58,
  82, 141
Anglo-French War (1790s), 76
Annapolis Convention (1786),
  66

Annapolis, Md. 6, 11, 18, 30, 31,
  42, 67, 85, 88, 91, 125, 126, 137
  Mayor's Court, 126
anti-Catholic attitudes *(see also*
  Nativism; Test Acts [British]),
  19
  Guy Fawkes Day, 55
Anti-Federalists (in 1790s) *(see*
  Democratic-Republican party)
Anti-Federalists (opponents of
  proposed U.S. Constitutions),
  35, 36, 37
  Archdiocese of, 101, 104, 113
Ariel (ship), 26
aristocracy, 70, 73, 182
Aristotle, 168
Articles of Confederation, 6, 11,
  17, 26, 27, 28, 31, 32, 60, 64, 66,
  68, 69, 72, 74, 87, 89, 91
assemblies, state *(see also* names
  of individual states), 12, 72, 74
Association of Freemen of
  Maryland, The, 85
atheism *(see also* religion) 76,
  177
Attorney General (Department
  of Justice) *(see* United States
  of America)
attorneys general, state *(see*
  names of individual states)
Augustinian Order, 63
Ave Maria (magazine), 184
Ayres, Captain, 52

B

Badin, Stephen, 110
Baker, Louisa, 9
Ballou, Adin, 165
Baltimore and Ohio Railroad, 14
Baltimore *Daily Advertiser,* 44
Baltimore Iron Works, 13
Baltimore, Lords, 7, 8
Baltimore, Md., 10, 14, 22, 23,
  88, 102, 104, 112, 129, 132, 133,
  136, 156,   210, 212
Bancroft, George, 169, 170, 180
Bank of Augusta v. Earle, 148,

229

justices *(see also* names of
individual justices), 1, 112,
121, 140, 143, 145, 146, 154,
156, 159, 196
"original package" doctrine,
134, 135
political questions, 150
slavery issue, 150, 154, 156
under Chief Justice Roger
Brooke Taney, 146-160
Supreme Executive council (of
U.S. during Revolutionary
War) *(see* United States of
America)
Susquehanna River, 14
Susquehannock Indians, 82
Sutter family, 189
Swain, David, 106
Swanwick, John, 76
Swisher, Carl Brent, 141
Sylvester, Peter, 38

T

Taggart, Joseph, 145
Taney family, 143
Taney Town, Md., 141
Taney, Anne Key, 126, 129, 141,
142
Taney, Augustus, 141
Taney, Dorothy, 141
Taney, Michael, 123, 124, 129
Taney, Mrs. Augustus, 141
Taney, Mrs. Michael (Roger
Brooke Taney's mother), 123,
141
Taney, Octavius, 141
Taney, Roger Brooke, 1, 156,
200, 209
ancestors were indentured
servants, 122
appointed by President
Jackson to be Chief Justice
of U.S. Supreme Court, 116
attitudes toward blacks
(Negroes), 143, 157-158
Attorney General of
Maryland, 134-135

Attorney General of the
United States, 135
birth and early life, 123-124
Brown v. Maryland case, 135
charitable actions, 142-145,
159-160
children reared as non-
Catholics, 142
commitment to Catholic
religion, 124, 141, 142, 145-
146, 158, 159
defeated in bid for reelection
to Maryland House of
Delegates in 1800, 129
Dred Scott v. Sandford
decision, 122, 140, 143, 146,
150, 151, 153-160
early legal career, 128, 129
early reluctance to defend
likely guilty clients, 127, 130,
131-132
education, 124-125
effect of Catholicism on
public life, 140
election campaign for House
of Delegates, 128
family members and family
life, 123-124, 126, 127, 129,
140-142, 146
highest ambition to become
Attorney General of
Maryland, 125
important cases during
practice in Frederick, Md.
(Buck, Williamson, and
Gruber cases), 130-131
influence of Dickinson
College on, 124
influence of father on, 123-
124
influence of mother on, 123
involved with state banks in
Maryland, 133
involvement in controversy
surrounding rechartering of
Second Bank of the United
States, 133, 135-140, 160
issue of Catholicism raised

About the Contributors

Rev. Thomas O'Brien Hanley, S.J., Ph.D. is Professor of History at Loyola College of Maryland and Editor and Biographer of The Carroll Papers. Perhaps the most prominent living authority on Charles Carroll of Carrollton, his books include *Charles Carroll of Carrollton: The Making of a Revolutionary Gentleman; Revolutionary Statesman: Charles Carroll and the War;* and *Their Rights and Liberties: The Beginnings of Religious and Political Freedom in Maryland.*

Dr. John J. Carrigg is Professor of History at Franciscan University of Steubenville, where he has been on the faculty for forty-five years. He previously taught history at Georgetown University. He authored a chapter in *American Secretaries of the Navy.* He has long been active in Republican party politics in Jefferson County, Ohio, and has served as President of the City Council in Steubenville, Ohio and Treasurer of Jefferson County.

Dr. Donald J. D'Elia is Professor of History at the State University of New York — College at New Paltz. He has also taught at Penn State University, Bloomsburg State College, Marist College, Dickinson College, and New York University. He has published numerous articles and has authored *The Spirits of '76: A Catholic Inquiry* (Christendom Press) and *Benjamin Rush: Philosopher of the American Revolution.* An active Secular Franciscan, he is also a charter member of the Fellowship of Catholic Scholars and a member of the Board of Advisors of both The Marian Institute for Advanced Studies and the Society of Catholic Social Scientists.

James R. Gaston is Assistant Professor of History and directs the Humanities and Catholic Culture Program at Franciscan University of Steubenville. He was an Earhart Foundation Fellow and served on the professional staff of the Intercollegiate Studies Institute for five years. He is on the Board of Directors of the Society of Catholic Social Scientists, and is a member of the American Historical Association and the Society for Christian Culture.

Dr. David M. Rooney is Associate Professor of Engineering at Hofstra University. He is also Chairman of the New York Catholic Forum. He has published articles and book reviews in *Faith & Reason, Fidelity,* and other Catholic publications. American Catholic history is his long-time avocation.

Dr. Stephen M. Krason, Esq. is Associate Professor of Political Science at Franciscan University of Steubenville. He has published numerous articles and book reviews and is the author of *Abortion: Politics, Morality, and the Constitution* and *Liberalism, Conservatism, and Catholicism*, the co-editor of *Parental Rights: The Contemporary Assault on Traditional Liberties* (Christendom Press), and the editor of *The Recovery of American Education*. The former Eastern Director of the Intercollegiate Studies Institute, he is President of The Marian Institute for Advanced Studies and a founder of the Society of Catholic Social Scientists.

Rev. Americo D. Lapati, Ph.D. is Rector of Our Lady of Providence Preparatory Seminary in Providence, Rhode Island. He previously taught at The Catholic University of America, Rhode Island College, and the University of Notre Dame. He is one of the leading scholars on Orestes A. Brownson in the U.S. Among his numerous published works is a book on Brownson's life in the Twayne's United States Authors Series and a new edition of Brownson's major work, *The American Republic*, which he edited. He has also written a book on Cardinal John Henry Newman in Twayne's English Authors Series.

Stuart Gudowitz is a professional librarian at George Washington University in Washington, D.C. He previously was on the professional library staff at the State University of New York — College at Buffalo and Cornell University. He has published articles and book reviews in such journals as *Fidelity*, *New Oxford Review*, and *Library Journal*.

CPSIA information can be obtained
at www.ICGtesting.com
Printed in the USA
LVHW011503160120
643871LV00002B/283